NEW TO BIG

NEW
TO
BIG

How Companies Can Create
Like Entrepreneurs, Invest Like VCs, and Install a
Permanent Operating System for Growth

David Kidder
AND Christina Wallace

CURRENCY
NEW YORK

Copyright © 2019 by TGOS LLC

Published in the United States by Currency,
an imprint of the Crown Publishing Group,
a division of Penguin Random House LLC, New York.
currencybooks.com

CURRENCY and its colophon are trademarks of Penguin Random House LLC.

Currency books are available at special discounts for bulk purchases for sales promotions or corporate use. Special editions, including personalized covers, excerpts of existing books, or books with corporate logos, can be created in large quantities for special needs. For more information, contact Premium Sales at (212) 572-2232 or e-mail specialmarkets@penguinrandomhouse.com.

Library of Congress Cataloging-in-Publication Data is available upon request.

ISBN 978-0-525-57359-3
Ebook ISBN 978-0-525-57360-9

PRINTED IN THE UNITED STATES OF AMERICA

Book design by Andrea Lau
Illustrations by Bionic
Jacket design by Rodrigo Corral Studio

10 9 8 7 6 5 4 3 2 1

First Edition

This book, and Bionic, would not exist if not for the imagination, instigation, and drive of two incredible women: Beth Comstock and our cofounder, Anne Berkowitch. This book is dedicated to you and to the entire Bionic tribe. We are beyond grateful.

Once Bionic, always Bionic.

Here's to the crazy ones . . . Because the people who are crazy enough to think they can change the world are the ones who do.

—Rob Siltanen

CONTENTS

1

NEW TO BIG

WHAT ARE YOU GOING TO DO WHEN THIS PARTNER-ship fails?" It was a simple question, but coming from two of the most respected and successful venture capital investors, Marc Andreessen and Ben Horowitz, it felt like a one-inch punch. They were doing due diligence before they invested in the Series C financing round of my four-year-old startup, Clickable, and I honestly did not have an answer. I had never considered that reality; I was going to will it to work. As if on cue, we all nervously laughed while I tried to keep my adrenaline under control.

As an entrepreneur, over the past twenty-odd years I have worked relentlessly and experienced modest success building several venture-backed startups. I have raised over $50 million in seed and growth capital and have exited twice. But a decade ago, at the moment Marc and Ben were doling out some radical candor, I was frozen with the realization that I had just made an irreversible, fatal decision in building my beloved startup.

Clickable was a pioneer in the search and social marketing space. We had discovered a real pain point: digital marketers had too many platforms to manage and too little understanding of which ones would actually move the needle. So we created and patented the Act Engine. It was a dashboard utilizing some of the earliest forms of machine learning to look across search and social campaigns and give marketers clarity on what to focus on each day.

We were in the right place at the right time and quickly raised over $22 million in our Series A and B financing rounds from some of the most respected venture capitalists in the world. But early on, we spotted a problem with our product-market fit. There were actually two groups of customers who needed us: large enterprises, who wielded the vast majority of online marketing spending, and smaller businesses, who felt the same pain but had much less money to spend on a solution.

The obvious fix would be to target the large enterprises; any entrepreneur will tell you their ideal customer is "rich and in pain." But our earliest revenue came from the smaller companies, and we were reluctant to abandon them and shift upmarket. As a result of being stuck in the "ugly teenage years," our growth rate had not yet met the exponential forecast required to raise another round of funding, and we were burning through capital quickly. It was a classic startup dilemma.

So when a Fortune 100 financial services company came knocking in 2009 with interest in pursuing a strategic partnership, we saw it as the silver bullet for our growth challenges. They were building a complete suite of digital marketing solutions for small- and medium-sized businesses, and our Act Engine fit perfectly into their strategy. They had paid a fortune to a prestigious consulting firm to analyze and recommend a leading technology partner, and the firm chose Clickable, resulting in a several-million-dollar partnership to launch a white-label version of our platform for their small-business customers. Unsurprisingly, their customers behaved exactly as our earliest customers did: they tried it, loved it, and then left it when the free trial was over because they couldn't afford to invest in the paid version. The "smartest plan you can buy" was invalidated. The partnership couldn't solve our problems; instead, it amplified them, which is exactly what Marc and Ben predicted. As serial founders and investors, they had hard-won experiences and critical answers that we severely required but did not yet possess.

Convinced we could still reboot Clickable's growth, I embarked on a quest to learn from the world's best (living) entrepreneurs. I wanted to understand how the most successful founders decided to bet their lives on a business, and then what they did in the first five years to keep those companies alive and thriving. What began as a series of conversations with entrepreneurs like Elon Musk, Reid Hoffman, Sara Blakely, Robin Chase, Steve Case, and more than forty other incredible founders, turned into my last book, *The Startup Playbook.*

What I learned was that while each founder's startup journey was unique, they all had a nearly identical collection of mind-sets and lenses they used to discover the root of a customer problem and to scale a solution into a business. These growth mind-sets were distilled into a framework I called the Five Lenses. (We'll dig into three of these lenses in chapter 7.)

Most entrepreneurs will tell you that the best ideas and the biggest opportunities are often discovered by someone in the right place at the right time, and in this particular story, that place and time was at the TED Conference in 2010, eating breakfast with Beth Comstock, then SVP and chief marketing and commercial officer of General Electric (GE). It was two years before I'd ultimately sell Clickable.

Beth and I had been friends for a decade, and our breakfast at TED was an annual affair, where we caught up on our various professional and family adventures in between presentations from some of the most creative and brilliant minds in art, technology, policy, and more. I was describing the Five Lenses from *The Startup Playbook* when Beth stopped me midsentence and insisted, "We need this learning at GE."

She had long owned the disrupter role at the conglomerate, leading their digital transformation efforts (including overseeing the founding of Hulu) and environmental impact work (including creating the Ecomagination initiative), and had recently stepped into the chief commercial officer role. She knew better than anyone that the core of the conglomerate struggled to be entrepreneurial, to operationalize the mind-sets and systems of growth. "Come work with me to install this at GE," she insisted.

I hesitated. I'm an entrepreneur, not a consultant, and at that point I had a deeply personal and moral commitment to my Clickable team and investors to cross the finish line, no matter the personal cost or the timeline ahead. So we put the idea on the shelf. But two years later, after we sold Clickable and just months before I published *The Startup Playbook*, Beth asked me to join her keynote panel at GE's Global Leadership Meeting in Boca Raton, Florida.

What I've learned from my experiences as a four-time entrepreneur and an angel investor in more than thirty startups is that while it often looks as if world-altering business opportunities emerge by accident, they can, in fact, be discovered and scaled in a methodical way. In the same way an MBA program teaches a form of management for administering and growing existing businesses, entrepreneurship and venture capital are, together, a form of management for discovering and building new businesses. And this is crucial: enterprises need both. It is the ecosystem created by the two that fuels world-changing innovation. This was the hard-earned, invaluable insight I gained from Clickable and our fatal Fortune 100 partnership. And what a gift it was. I needed to share this insight at the GE Global Leadership meeting.

The challenge would be how to introduce this new ethos and system into a traditional corporate environment. Existing corporations are focused on operational excellence and incremental improvements through process and efficiency. The MBA-driven methodology they use is about taking something big and making it bigger. It is, literally, the toolkit for operating what we call the Big to Bigger machine. Conversely, the integrated mind-set, mechanics, and methodologies of entrepreneurship and venture capital are designed and calibrated to discover new customer needs and devise innovative and new-to-the-world solutions. It is the toolkit of the New to Big machine.

What Beth had been articulating about GE—their struggle to innovate inside their Big to Bigger machine—was an issue plaguing virtually every large organization and enterprise. GE didn't have a monopoly on this problem; it was everywhere. Corporate innovation is failing at a DNA level because the Big to Bigger machine has been engineered to be incompatible with New to Big. It is literally at war with growth. Truly new, cutting-edge ideas are too risky, too amorphous, too non-consensus to survive the metrics and evaluation process that "well-run" companies apply to capital investments.

Bionic was born at GE's conference in Boca. It was not intended, but it happened with a single provocative question. Near the end of the session, Beth surprised the three panelists by asking us onstage if we had any questions as outsiders to the company. Off the cuff, I aimed a question from the stage down to then CEO Jeffrey Immelt, who was seated front row center in an audience of seven hundred executives: "Jeff, how many fifty-million-dollar startups did GE launch last year?" The room shifted uncomfortably. "I bet the answer is zero," I continued. "And if that's true, I would be terrified if I were you. With ninety billion dollars in the bank and three hundred thousand employees, how does this not happen all the time?"

The silence was deafening.

Finally, Beth, stunned, broke the chill in the room with humor: "Tell us how you really feel!" The audience golf-clapped as I walked offstage, and I was certain my unintended, three-hour career as a "thought leader" had just been nuked. Instead Jeff closed the annual conference with a bold statement: "That was the most important question in the history of this leadership conference."

By the time I left Boca, I had agreed to partner with Beth. Over the next year, my initial work with GE was a series of keynotes on growth and startup mind-sets, alongside the brilliant thought leader Eric Ries, who was scaling his Lean Startup framework for enterprises. This work quickly expanded to Boeing and Tyco with an early version of Bionic's Validation methodology (something akin to a startup accelerator with lean experimentation mechanics).

As the demand grew, I saw a need for a more robust New to Big "operating system," so to speak. So, with entrepreneurs Anne Berkowitch and Rick Smith and a handful of my core Clickable team, I cofounded a new company, Bionic, to create just that. Over the past six years, we have worked with over a dozen partners, including Citigroup, Procter & Gamble, Nike, Exelon, Microsoft, and others. We've bootstrapped to over seventy-five fellow entrepreneurs, early-stage investors, and gifted product creators to help Bionic advance and refine this growth operating system (or Growth OS, as we call it). The Growth OS pairs the mind-sets, tools, and platforms of entrepreneurship with those of venture capital, and supports this ecosystem with the organizational systems enterprises need in order to work at the speed, cost, and competitiveness of startups. It has become a powerful, integrated way to unlock growth.

After six years of successfully installing the Growth OS into more than a dozen Fortune 500 partners, we wanted to share some key learnings. These are insights that I believe are relevant to anyone searching for growth, whether you work in a large enterprise or a regional nonprofit, whether you are the CEO of a mature SMB or a middle manager who wants to understand what keeps your senior leadership up at night.

Here are some of the headlines:

Are big organizations screwed when it comes to innovation?

In a word: no.

They just have to recognize the need to build a separate New to Big machine to run in tandem with their established Big to Bigger way of working. New to Big discovers, validates, and grows new ideas into big businesses, say $50 million or so. Big to Bigger takes those $50 million businesses and scales them to $500 million or more, leveraging the customers, manufacturing, distribution, and brand of the enterprise—the core strength of Big to Bigger. Ultimately, the success of New to Big sits squarely with the CEO. It's not a money, ideas, or talent problem; it's a permission and ownership problem, and it starts at the top.

How do you plan for growth in this New to Big machine?

The surprising answer: You don't. At least, not in the linear, blueprint planning model most of you are probably thinking about. Growth must be discovered; then you can "steer" toward it using what we call a portfolio approach.

The future technologies, trends, and markets are not yet known, and they are changing far too fast for a traditional business-planning approach. The future looks nothing like the past, and relying on old expertise, old data, and old insights will only ensure expensive failure. So instead of sinking large amounts of capital into a select few new ventures, often called rack-and-stack planning, companies need to embrace the power of portfolios—placing dozens of small bets, using the tools of discovery and validation to reveal which ones will be successful. Angel and venture capitalists do this innately, and large enterprises can adopt their playbook. **This is fundamentally about learning velocity, and whoever learns the fastest wins.**

> Can you apply New to Big methodology to a product or service that's already in development in a company?

Yes. But you have to be prepared to learn that you may need to kill it instead (even if it's already in market).

First you need to make sure that the product or service in development is addressing your *customer's* problem, rather than solving *your own* problem. Market-making innovation isn't about you. It's about the problems or needs in the world that you are strategically positioned to address. Look outside your own walls and pay attention to the new behaviors, shifting market forces, and emerging technologies that will define both what you build and how you build it. You must reorient from "inside out" to "outside in" to discover growth. You'll never find disruptive growth in internal, consensus-driven beliefs.

Everything you'll read about here is based on a combination of research, decision science, the expertise of our advisors and partners, and our own firsthand experiences working with Fortune 500 companies. My team and I sought to create a resource that captures our methods, explains them in plain language, and empowers all readers to ponder, experiment with, and apply them in ways that truly suit their organizations. This book was written by Bionic as a team, and brilliantly orchestrated and captured by my partner, Christina Wallace.

In general, we tried to keep things fairly high-level. We dig into a few tactics, but don't want to bog you down with too many details. We give you the scaffolding and let you decide how to erect the needed structure in your organization. We are convinced that the refounding of iconic companies—including the development of the next generation of growth leaders within those companies—is the most significant opportunity and the greatest leadership challenge of our era. This is why we built Bionic. In this book, Christina and I are giving you the tools and encourage you to use them in ways that will complement your specific business model and growth goals.

Now, if you'd like a bit of historical context on why real, market-making innovation is so difficult for companies across all industries, dig into chapter 2. But if you want to get started fast, skip to chapter 3, where we'll outline the first set of crucial mind-set shifts you'll need to tackle at your own organization.

Either way, welcome. Welcome to what I hope will be a powerful, accessible, and inspiring tool to install an always-on, permanent capability for growth. Welcome to the power of New to Big.

2

HOW WE GOT HERE

IN 2001 THE LIST OF COMPANIES WITH THE HIGHEST market caps was dominated by blue chips. GE, Microsoft, Exxon-Mobil, Walmart, and Citigroup—all were businesses led by managers who had mastered efficiency and optimization and who grew their businesses by making them work better than they had previously. Fast-forward to the present, and the list looks strikingly different. As of this writing, Apple, Amazon, Alphabet, Microsoft, and Facebook now top the list, with Tencent and Alibaba close behind. They are, for the most part, young firms led by founders and their teams, driven by bold, first-generation leaders who continually prioritize new growth over efficiencies in their core businesses.

Many things have happened in the intervening years to contribute to this shift, but the signal is undeniable. The market now rewards these pioneering enterprises and supports their vision and continual investment in new growth. Large enterprises have been attempting to respond to these developments for some time, mainly by applying the methods of startups, such as lean experimentation, design thinking, and agile development. But the focus on entrepreneurial tactics without a shift in our leadership mind-set is merely a Band-Aid on the problem.

Before we can dive into better ways to address new growth, we have to understand how the efficiency mind-set came to rule the business world—and how it was neither inevitable nor all that effective.

CAPITALISM AS PATRIOTISM

Privately held corporations of the late 1800s were run by the families that founded them. Back when Carnegies and Rockefellers dominated the earth, legacy sons, regardless of their interest levels or skill sets, nearly always inherited moneymaking empires from their fathers. Lower-ranking employees were hired in, but the top brass was all family.

Although it may sound positively quaint now, back then both family-run and civic-minded corporations were expected to build their businesses in ways that supported their communities. Since the American government created a fertile environment for corporate growth and prosperity, organizations benefiting from that environment were advised to behave with grace and gratitude.[1] These companies were designed to care for employees, customers, and stockholders in almost equal measure.

This attitude remained fairly ubiquitous, even as the families who owned large corporations began to hand off their oversight to professional managers. But by the early 1930s, economists began saying that keeping management separate from ownership was essential to long-term success. The era that followed is often referred to as "managerial capitalism," a time in which the piloting of be-hemoth organizations shifted from owner-founders to hired guns.[2]

Many of these newly minted CEOs and executives took it upon themselves to streamline the organizations they ran. Between the 1930s and the 1950s, the American economy had very limited available capital, which meant corporate leaders tried to squeeze the maximum amount of profit from every dollar spent. Business school had taught them it was perfectly fine to freely use resources that were abundant and cheap, but rare and costly resources needed to be meticulously stewarded. Liquid cash was scarce at the time, so only investments that paid off handsomely were considered success-ful. And success was no longer measured as straight profit in dol-lars, but instead as ratios like RONA (return on net assets), ROCE (return on capital employed), and IRR (internal rate of return).[3] Waste became the ultimate enemy, and efficiency the ultimate goal.

Yet even as leadership structures and organizational priorities changed, core values remained rock-solid. Well into the 1950s and '60s, corporations built factories on their home turf, invested in real innovation that churned out life-changing products, created mil-lions of jobs that fueled the middle class, paid billions in taxes, and enthusiastically worked to fortify the American economy in virtu-ally every way.[4] Early CEOs championed this philosophy.

Then economists began to grumble. And their grumblings changed everything.

THE SHIFT TO SHAREHOLDER GRATIFICATION

In 1967, economist John Kenneth Galbraith catalyzed a business-world shake-up by publishing *The New Industrial State*. In this book, he posits that American mega-corporations had grown too powerful and were no longer truly serving public or consumer needs. He said these companies fabricated markets through manipulative advertising, and focused on accumulating cash instead of fixing customer problems.[5] Galbraith sowed the seeds of mistrust in corporate America, but what sprouted from them was surprising.

Economists Michael C. Jensen and William H. Meckling also became outraged, but on behalf of a different population. Where Galbraith wanted executives to answer to customers and the American public, Jensen and Meckling believed they should answer to stockholders. To understand why, we need to rewind a few decades.

The American economy had experienced a much-needed economic boom in the years following World War II. During this "golden" age, many corporations were raking in profits so huge that they never had to concern themselves with choosing whom to please; there was enough to go around, and stakeholders, employees, and communities were all happy and handsomely paid. But by the late 1960s, globalization and deregulation began to have huge impacts on the American economic landscape. Increased competition meant smaller profit margins, and executives could no longer spread company wealth around so freely. Ultimately, they determined it was better to disappoint shareholders than to give short shrift to workers or customers.[6]

By the mid-'70s—after a decade of unremarkable profits and negative returns—shareholder disappointment turned into indignation. Investors were weary of seeing stocks that had long been profitable suddenly lose value, and incensed that companies seemed to be doing little to rectify the situation. Sensing growing unrest, powerful economists began to demand a change in business priorities.

In 1976, Jensen and Meckling led the charge by publishing an incendiary paper titled "Theory of the Firm: Managerial Behavior, Agency Costs and Ownership Structure" in the *Journal of Financial Economics*. This now legendary piece served as an angry rebuke to the entire philosophy of managerial capitalism. These two venerable economists claimed that any corporations built to serve customer needs and reward professional managers were wrecking the economy. They further asserted that these organizations were shirking their responsibility to produce returns for their shareholders.[7]

And the accusations didn't stop there. Jensen and Meckling claimed that CEOs and managers could not be trusted to work on behalf of shareholders, since they were far too consumed with padding their own bank accounts. Galbraith's ideas in *The New Industrial State* supported this supposition by pointing out that most companies concentrated on the gradual refinement of their products, not on boosting their stock prices. A company that built cars or produced cheese or manufactured circuit boards wasn't designed to devise tactics that yielded more money for shareholders. The people working inside those companies aimed their efforts at producing more and better cars, cheeses, and circuit boards.[8] Which meant that, in essence, no one was looking out for shareholder profits.

The battle cry resonated, and soon more and more corporations were hearing from incensed stockholders demanding better market performance. CEOs recognized that they needed to "maximize shareholder value" or risk losing their jobs. Executives became convinced that they answered to and worked for their shareholders. And as we moved into the 1980s, corporate boards took on the task of getting managerial and shareholder interests into alignment, often by rewarding executives with stock-based bonuses as motivators.[9] Shareholders, once an afterthought, were now a vocal and powerful economic force.

As Cornell Law professor Lynn Stout points out in her 2012 book, *The Shareholder Value Myth*, there were no laws in place that forced executives to fulfill shareholders' fiduciary expectations. Executives pledged allegiance to the corporation itself, and were expected to act in its best interests. Shareholders were contractually entitled to the "residual value" of the corporation after its other financial obligations had been fulfilled, but nowhere did any doctrine state that corporate leadership must actively work to boost that residual value.[10] This was not an encoded shift, but instead a tacit agreement between CEOs and investors. And it was an agreement that persists to this day.

THE ILLUSION OF GROWTH

This sea change transformed both the economy and the stock market. In the 1960s, 10 percent of households controlled 90 percent of US corporate stocks. By the 1980s—after the shift toward shareholder appeasement—pension funds, mutual funds, and institutional investors controlled 60 percent of stocks. Additionally, hedge fund managers craving hefty quarterly returns changed the very nature of investing. Through the 1960s, people tended to buy stock and hold on to it. The number of shares bought and sold on the New York Stock Exchange—a phenomenon called "turnover"—averaged a mere 20 percent per year.[11] With the new focus on fast-turn profits and obsession with quarterly numbers, the 1980s saw turnover rates climb above 70 percent. An average stock was held by fund managers for just twelve months.[12] If a stock wasn't performing on a quarterly basis, fund managers dumped it without a second thought. (And dumping stocks continues to be a popular activity: In 2015, turnover rates hovered around 150 percent.[13])

This meant that within company walls, leaders were driven to generate short-term wins that brought incremental shareholder returns. Delivering the best solutions to consumers and upholding responsibilities to employees, suppliers, and communities dropped off their collective radar. Any activity that failed to nudge stock prices ever upward was deprioritized and abandoned.

Leadership teams still relied on efficiency-focused ratios to measure success, but they found clever ways to manipulate those ratios to their advantage. Since RONA, ROIC, and IRR are fractions, they can be tweaked by making changes to either the numerator *or* the denominator. Generating more profit would add to the numerator, driving RONA or ROIC up. But new growth is harder than cutting costs, so naturally, more executives turned to cost cutting to reduce the denominator, which had the same net effect of increasing the overall ratio. IRR could be boosted by adding profit to the numerator, or by championing projects that paid off quickly and reduced the denominator.[14] This system of (perfectly legal) cleverness meant that companies didn't have to grow real-world profits in order to satisfy shareholders' collective hunger for returns. They just had to reduce expenditures and boost their ratios.

Then efficiency went from a priority to a craze with the birth of Six Sigma. With roots in German mathematics[15] and refinements made during the rebuilding of Japan after World War II,[16] this set of ideals was distilled by Motorola leadership in 1986 and transformed into a wildly popular management method. Executives who followed Six Sigma were urged to focus on statistical analysis and measurable process improvements instead of driving innovation or conquering new markets. As the 1980s rolled into the early 1990s, more and more corporations began adopting these tactics, fueling a bona fide efficiency epidemic. Companies looked inward more and more, determined to save costs and boost shareholder value without actually making anything new or addressing consumer pain points.

Initially, economists believed this new era of efficiency-obsessed leadership would lead to nonstop innovation. But with quarterly returns constantly looming, all innovative energies were directed toward tweaking existing systems to make them more efficient and more profitable. The result was that leaders, shareholders, and fund managers began to view corporations as bundles of financial assets instead of groups of people generating ideas and meeting customer needs. And when a company's value is boiled down to its assets, there's no reason to prioritize customer satisfaction or product management. It's all about the balance sheets.[17] Why pour cash into investigating a new market when you can just wring profits from your existing market?

Eventually, it became clear that shareholder pressure didn't just encourage consistent quarterly results, it actively *discouraged* R&D, new growth efforts, innovation, and exploration. Not only that, but the focus on boosting stocks didn't actually yield the desired results for shareholders; stock returns during this period were statistically worse than they'd been before "shareholder value" became the top priority.[18]

Corporations of every stripe bent over backward to increase shareholder returns, overhauling processes and eradicating creativity along the way, and *still* couldn't deliver. Which brings us to the digital age, when the internet fundamentally changed the ability of small companies to reach customers and new business models would eventually shatter long-held beliefs about success, profitability, and growth. Business cycles were speeding up at a dizzying rate and enterprises began to see the risk of not keeping up.

STARTUP SHAKEDOWN

Now we're edging toward more familiar territory, including events that many of us witnessed firsthand. But let's do a quick recap so we're all on the same page.

Starting in the late 1990s, internet and tech companies began to proliferate and flourish. Online commerce became a driver of massive growth, spawning retailers who hawked everything from books to shoes to food to consumer services over the internet. Investors were thrilled by this emerging market and ravenously snapped up stocks from frequent and lucrative IPOs. The NASDAQ soared, and many people got very, very rich.[19] But in March 2000, the bubble burst, and dozens of companies that had been Wall Street darlings folded overnight. This happened for a number of reasons, but the main one was that *many of these companies didn't have sound business models.*[20] Investors were betting on the startups' ability to get into the black eventually, but the market reached critical mass and crashed before many of them could even begin to earn.

Despite its disastrous repercussions, the Dot-Com Boom also laid some important groundwork. Over the next ten to fifteen years, entrepreneurs learned how to build and scale businesses quickly and to take ideas from whiteboard to market faster than their predecessors ever dreamed possible. They focused on identifying a customer need or friction point and devising a service or product that solved the problem in a way that was radically new. They eschewed shareholder returns in favor of utility and innovation. They plunged fearlessly into new markets and made big waves with small amounts of capital. Tech and online startups changed the game. And for the most part, they changed it for the better.

As we mentioned at the beginning of this chapter, 2001's top five companies by market capitalization were GE, Microsoft, Exxon-Mobil, Citigroup, and Walmart. By mid-2018, they were Apple, Amazon, Alphabet, Microsoft, and Facebook. It's not hard to see the trend in those lineups. Traditional big enterprise tumbled right off the list, and all the top spots now belong to technology companies who are obsessed with solving customer problems rather than delivering shareholder value.

You've probably noticed that Microsoft made it onto the Market Cap Honor Roll in both 2001 and 2018. It's worth noting that it actually dropped off the list in the intervening years, but is currently in a rather spectacular state of reemergence. And that all comes down to leadership.

Microsoft lost its mojo when cofounder Bill Gates stepped down in 2000 and staid executive Steve Ballmer took over the CEO role. While other tech firms were on a tear, Microsoft languished with a series of "me-too" product launches and a protectionist view of their cash cows, Windows and Microsoft Office.[21] But in 2014, a new CEO was appointed, one who behaved with the conviction and passion of a startup founder while piloting an industry giant. And in just a few years, Satya Nadella has made remarkable progress toward righting the ship.[22] What's he bringing to the table that his predecessor couldn't? A mind-set shift.

In a 2015 interview with The Verge about the future of Microsoft, Nadella said, "We no longer talk about the lagging indicators of success—revenue, profit. What are the leading indicators of success? Customer love."[23] In his book *Hit Refresh: The Quest to Rediscover Microsoft's Soul and Imagine a Better Future for Everyone*, he outlines a very startup-reminiscent philosophy of promoting exciting new ideas, creating spaces for employees to try and fail, and keeping an eye on long-term goals instead of fretting over quarterly returns. Nadella has taken over a company that began as a startup, grew into an entrenched behemoth, and is now on its way toward a successful hybridization of established corporate structure with entrepreneurial business tactics. And with double-digit profit margin growth every quarter since 2017, it's clear his tactics are working.[24] You could credibly claim that Nadella has *refounded* Microsoft.

More CEOs will need to follow suit. Growth leaders must stop focusing their energies on incremental growth through endless optimization, and instead leverage their companies' assets to build new offerings, move into new markets, and create next-generation solutions. When a CEO with that growth mind-set takes the wheel at a legacy company, dazzling change suddenly becomes possible.

THE NEXT PHASE

Every year, BlackRock founder Larry Fink pens a letter to all the CEOs who head companies in which his clients have invested. In 2016, he used this letter to inform all five hundred of them that he was no longer interested in investing in companies who were gamifying their share prices through stock buybacks (illegal until the early 1980s) and short-term fixes. Instead, he said, he wanted to use his then $5.1 trillion in assets under management to invest in companies that had a genuine obsession with customer value.[25]

Then Fink stepped it up a notch: His 2018 annual shareholder letter insisted that financial performance, no matter how exceptional, was no longer enough to warrant his capital. He wanted to invest in companies that were serving a social purpose. Yet he insisted he wasn't abandoning capitalism. Rather—given the shifting mood of the country, and outside forces like policy changes in taxes, immigration, and LGBTQ rights—companies without a sense of purpose "will ultimately lose the license to operate from key stakeholders." (Research conducted by Julie Battilana, founder and faculty chair of the Social Innovation and Change Initiative at Harvard Kennedy School, shows that when companies heed social issues, they actually outperform companies that focus solely on boosting stock prices.[26])

So now enterprises need to focus not only on customer value, but also on showcasing how they are contributing to society, all while staring down Wall Street's pressure for quarterly performance. It's no wonder they're desperate for a new way to work.

These new mandates breed new questions: How do you plan ten to fifteen years into the future? How do you discover new problems and needs your enterprise is uniquely positioned to address? How do you break the incremental growth cycle and reignite innovation? Our answer? By deploying a new form of management that is specifically designed to deal with the unknowable and is built around customer needs.

In *The Startup Way*, Lean Startup champion Eric Ries called startups an "atomic unit of work for highly uncertain terrain."[27] At their core, startups are a way of working that discovers and validates solutions to customer problems. And that's the vital first piece of the puzzle, but startups can't exist in a vacuum. They require a funding mechanism, which is where venture capital comes in. We've realized that, together, they form a powerful ecosystem for discovering new solutions and nurturing them into big businesses.

At Bionic, we believe that enterprises can deploy entrepreneurship and venture capital as a form of growth management.

We understand why some corporate leaders are at first hesitant to adopt this methodology. They often point out that startups have very little at risk, since they're so small and so new. Big companies have processes that were refined over decades of work, via thousands of employees, and on behalf of millions of customers. A radical shift from tweaking existing products and streamlining proven processes to exploring new markets is more than uncomfortable—it's terrifying. But the startup mentality isn't meant to replace existing business functions, it's meant to complement them.

At Bionic we created the Growth OS to function like a smaller, New to Big machine that runs in tandem alongside the gargantuan, Big to Bigger machine. This is important: The Growth OS feeds the primary enterprise, but doesn't replace it. Instead this (metaphorical) operating system leverages the mind-sets, mechanics, and tools of the startup ecosystem to ignite growth revolutions inside enterprises.

The competitive advantages that big companies have over startups are experience and scale. When C-level execs at a Fortune 500 company pick up on a trend or identify a ripe new customer need, they've already got the means to pursue and accelerate. They have customers, distribution, supply chain, and a trustworthy brand already lined up. Because of this, they can make or break fringe ideas and experimental products. If J.P.Morgan decides to get on board with Bitcoin, that will give this emerging currency instant legitimacy. They have the scale and relationships to do that. They have the necessary gravitas.

The competitive advantages that startups have over big companies are greater speed and lower cost of learning. A decision that takes Unilever six months to solidify via committee discussions and executive sign-offs may take Brandless six days.

The Growth OS combines the best of both worlds. It takes the agility and creativity of startups and weaves them with the expertise and clout of corporate legacy. Following our blueprint, established companies can recapture their growth skills. They already know how to grow from Big to Bigger. What we teach is a new and necessary skill set: how to foster growth from New to Big.

So now that we all understand how we got here, let's get going.

3

FROM TAM TO TAP

IMAGINE THAT YOU SCOUT, TRAIN, AND MANAGE OLYMpic athletes. You've got an eye for potential and a nose for talent, so you can watch a collegiate high diver perform and know for certain that person could bring home armloads of gold medals. You come on board once the athlete has already done most of her growing and a large part of her training, and you transform her into an unbeatable, world-class competitor. You know how to predict the results you'll get based on the effort you invest, and you know how to measure your success. You take something big, and make it bigger.

Now let's say a trusted colleague comes to you with a gifted five-year-old and says, "Make this kid into an Olympian." You're completely out of your depth, and you know it. You have no clue how to motivate someone this young, even if he's off-the-charts talented. And even if you *were* able to measure how fast he could run or how high he could jump *right now,* those metrics would be meaningless in a few short months. But your colleague has set you to a task, and you want to help. So what do you do?

You call on early childhood experts, teachers, and loving parents who have raised Olympians. You say, "Teach him and nurture him and call me when he's graduated from college and ready to train for the Olympics." You are simply not skilled to deal with New to Big. You can lead Big to Bigger like a world-class coach, but this? Not your expertise.

Of course, if you asked those early childhood experts, teachers, and loving parents to guide a pole vaulter for nationals and onto the world stage, they too would be useless. They're all about New to Big, but they'd fail miserably at Big to Bigger.

USING STARTUP TACTICS TO MANAGE THE NEW

Startups know how to identify, address, and fulfill customer needs. Almost every captivating startup origin story involves entrepreneurs recognizing a point of friction and thinking, *There must be a better way!* This fixation on problem-solving is the key to groundbreaking entrepreneurship. By starting with the customer pain point, entrepreneurs give themselves boundless permission and flexibility to dream up and experiment with solutions. The best option might be a product, or a service, or a way of merging existing products or services into an integrated solution. Regardless of how diverse the array of possible solutions may be, startups keep their options wide open, experimenting and tweaking until they land on a solution that meets customer needs in a radically new way. Instead of battling with competitors over market share, they simply create new markets. (There's a saying in Silicon Valley that "competition is for losers.") And because they are small and nimble, startups can experiment and change direction quickly and cheaply, with incredible learning velocity.

Established companies, on the other hand, know how to grow market share, increase profits, and refine existing processes and systems. They usually have the customer base, distribution, and supply chain to ensure their products and services reach customers reliably and with a high level of quality control. They may be old school, but they're *damned good* at what they do. As a result, they see no reason to ponder ideas that fall outside their comfort zones; they view the world through a lens they've built themselves, and one that tends to turn ideas inward. When it comes to brainstorming new products, they typically start with their own pain points, like: "We're losing market share; our margins are shrinking; we have a technology, now let's go find a customer for it." And that's when "old school" downshifts into obsolescence.

Yet this thinking doesn't exist in a vacuum. Legacy companies operate this way because they're hardwired to do so: Enterprises are in the "knowable" business but are at a loss when dealing in the "unknowable." With pressure from the street on stock prices and financial measures of success, the mere *thought* of investing in customer problems with unforeseeable results makes them incredibly uncomfortable. They're running a low-variation and low-risk incremental machine, and being told by leadership and shareholders to keep that machine humming along *or else.*

This inside-out thinking must change. The twenty-first century's most engrossing business success stories all stem from outside-in thinking; identifying the massive, global problems or needs that a company's unique gifts can solve. And it's time for the rest of us to adopt that problem-solving mind-set. If we want to catalyze exponential growth, we need to quit investigating how many people might buy our 10 percent improved widget and start identifying which big problems in the world we are perfectly positioned to solve.

We need to allow ourselves to look beyond what we've already done and imagine freely what we *can* do. The way we do this is by shifting from a Total Addressable Market (or TAM) model, which is based on planning in a known, share-based world, to a Total Addressable Problem (or TAP) model, which is based on discovering a brand-new customer problem or need.

The TAM framework is one that's been around for decades, and countless businesses rely on it to guide their decision-making processes. It addresses the question of how big a market is, and how large a share of that market a company can reasonably command (or "address"). This worldview is effective for markets that are knowable and already exist, but it's useless for markets that haven't been discovered or created yet. And that's where we're aiming our sights.

The TAP framework, on the other hand, takes a totally different approach: identifying a significant customer problem, working backward from the outside in to define a solution, and crafting a business model for that solution. Shifting from TAM to TAP helps us discover the big problems we can solve and uncover the new markets we can create.

Let's take a look at an example: mobile phones.

When they first came onto the consumer market, it seemed like the only people who'd want mobile phones were lawyers and high-powered executives. The perceived TAM was relatively small: "People in high-pressure jobs with time-sensitive communications needs who can afford a mobile office." But as the technology became lighter, faster, smaller, and more affordable, demand grew exponentially. Electronics designers recognized that mobile phones were addressing a much larger customer need—allowing *all* people to communicate on the go—and shifted gears to accommodate this new market. Very few people foresaw that future generations of these devices would eventually replace pagers, then replace landlines, and then become primary modes of connectivity for whole populations. It turns out that the TAP was literally the potential market size of "mobile communication."

Here's a more recent example: If you were a VC with the opportunity to invest in Facebook in 2003 and were convinced their TAM was "college students at Ivy League schools who want to stay connected," you would certainly have passed on the deal. That market size just wasn't big enough for the kind of returns you needed in your fund. But, of course, you'd be kicking yourself today. Because the site's phenomenal growth stemmed from its founders' understanding that the platform they'd built could do more and be more to a much broader population. They knew that people outside of college campuses wanted to know what their friends, colleagues, and family members were up to; that phone calls and emails weren't sufficiently keeping people connected; and that human curiosity was a powerful driver of online behavior. They had stumbled upon a previously unaddressed need, and they built a market around it. What was initially seen as "Friendster for college kids" grew to become a social media colossus. It turns out that the TAP was "staying connected with your extended personal network, asynchronously."

Neither of these ideas was conceived to steal market share from a competitor. Both of these ideas started out addressing a small and specialized audience, but grew to serve a much larger one. It wasn't "We made this thing. Who needs it?" It was "How could we meet the needs of a larger group of potential customers?" And that's how we all need to start thinking.

INVEST IN PROBLEMS, NOT PROJECTS

Now that we've trash-talked TAM, let's take a step back and discuss how it is still useful to anyone within our companies engaged in growth work. The TAM worldview isn't inherently wrong; in fact, TAM makes sense for existing markets, existing customers, and existing behaviors. It functions within the domain of the knowable: how much do customers currently spend for solutions in this market? For example, if we were in the lip gloss business and wanted to expand into lipstick, we could use TAM to estimate how big the market is and how much of it we might reasonably be able to address.

But once we head into the unknown, TAM loses its authority. Since we're in brand-new territory, the questions we would ask to determine TAM become impossible to answer, and we're forced to consider new questions: Is this a new customer behavior or point of friction? Are customers currently solving the problem or just now noticing the pain point? How many customers might need to solve this problem someday? If a solution that is better, faster, or cheaper were available, how might that change who can and will solve this problem? Looking at it from this perspective, we're able to see the size of the opportunity (TAP) instead of the market size of existing solutions (TAM). And by starting with problems, we don't confine ourselves to products; we open ourselves up to a whole universe of potential solutions.

To look strategically toward 2030 and beyond, we have to acknowledge that future markets, business models, and technologies are largely unknowable. This means any attempt at a *planning* strategy will fail, because the target is undefined. Instead we need to use a *discovery* strategy to uncover new customer behaviors, new needs, and emerging or nonexistent markets: new areas of opportunity (or Opportunity Areas—OAs—as we call them).

When we choose to shift focus from products to problems, the magnitude and variety of potential solutions skyrockets. And when we consider which new business enablers can be brought to bear against those problems at the places where problems and enablers intersect, then we can find OAs. (More on the nuts and bolts of this process in chapter 5.)

For an OA to be viable, it must encompass both a widespread need and a technology or solution that addresses that need in a radically different, substantially better way. The need should be something that never changes, but the products or services or solutions that address that need will change over time. And when we position our companies at the intersections of those needs and those new enabling solutions, we position ourselves for innovation. Standing at that crossroads, we can choose to move our businesses in new directions, create and conquer new markets, and pioneer world-changing solutions to vast and persistent problems.

But to get to that crossroads, we can't start with an existing market. We have to force ourselves to get comfortable with the unknowable, with markets that don't exist yet. We have to start with a need, gauge how many people currently use solution proxies, consider viable enablers, and unlock a whole set of possible solutions.

To see this process in action, let's unpack a case study.

OAS IN ACTION: TD AMERITRADE

TD Ameritrade is a brokerage firm with a forty-year legacy of providing investing services and education to individuals and custodial services to independent registered investment advisors. In 2017, company leadership made a push to increase their innovation capacity. They ran a series of innovation sprints that granted participants wide-open boundaries to explore how TD Ameritrade could deliver on its purpose to "transform lives and investing for the better."

One idea at their first innovation sprint rose to the top; everyone agreed it was a game-changer. The team that came up with the idea explored possible solutions and created a data-driven digital tool that, when pitched to senior leaders, received unanimous support from the executive team. At one point during the pitch the CEO, Tim Hockey, asked everyone in the room, "Who would want to use this tool?" Nearly every hand shot up. Some market research following the sprint confirmed the viability of this project; when potential customers were asked if they wanted (and would pay for) the tool, the answer was a resounding yes!

When the sprint concluded, TD Ameritrade leadership decided to use this potential game changer as a test case for an Opportunity Area. A three-person team was formed to focus on it, keeping one of the sprint participants and adding two new cofounders with fresh perspectives.

With new minds and permission to pursue the idea "for real," the cofounders took a step back from the solution itself and examined the underlying assumptions: Who was the customer, and what problem did they need to solve? How big was this problem, and what other solutions were these customers using currently? Was this problem growing or shrinking? And what were the new enablers (technologies, trends, etc.) that could be applied to solve the problem?

They started with the largest, most obvious customer persona and employed several rounds of experiments to refine their understanding of the need at hand. But their initial customer profile wasn't panning out; the customers they sought out were happy with the tools they were already using. So the team looked at adjacent personas. After all, the customers in the initial experiments kept saying, "I don't need this, but I know someone else who does," usually a close friend or family member.

But these adjacent customers didn't feel they had a problem and weren't seeking a solution. Perhaps the tool would be "nice to have," but when it came down to demonstrating how they would use it, they balked at the effort required. Over the course of five or six rounds of experiments that touched more than fifty potential customers, the three cofounders came to realize "there was no *there* there."

One of the cofounders, Matt, came from a data analytics background and was initially skeptical that they could invalidate an entire Opportunity Area with only a few dozen data points. "With my background, I typically want to collect thousands of data points to be sure of something. But I learned that you can talk to ten people and invalidate something. By talking with customers directly, I realized we could learn the answer fast and feel comfortable invalidating it and moving forward."

It took the team less than two weeks from kicking off the work to invalidating the Opportunity Area with confidence. But they also knew the CEO and entire senior leadership had raised their hands in support of the project back at the innovation sprint. So they kept looking. What if they had missed something? They couldn't go back with their findings until they knew with certainty.

To be sure they covered all the potential customer personas that might be attracted to this tool, they devised a quantitative survey. Maybe the problem wasn't the obvious one they initially identified; maybe the tool could meet a more niche need. They pivoted several times, eliminating some needs that were too small to be viable and others that were already being well served by a crowded marketplace of solutions. After five weeks, the cofounders were certain: The Opportunity Area was invalidated. Now they just had to tell the CEO. Cofounder Sarah commented, "We were confident in our findings, but nervous about telling the story."

The team gathered the evidence and learnings they had collected along the way. They had invalidated this particular tool and the broader customer problem it aimed to solve, but in the process, the team had uncovered a handful of new customer problems that looked promising. Cofounder Susan shared, "One of the things we did really well in that storytelling was talk about the unexpected needs we found. We uncovered needs that were really compelling and that we could address."

Tim Hockey and the entire executive team accepted the team's evidence, even though it directly contradicted their gut reaction during the initial pitch, and celebrated how quickly and cheaply the team had invalidated the Opportunity Area. If the team had explored the viability of this tool using a market analysis to calculate TAM, the executive team could easily have decided to make a big investment and built a product nobody would actually buy or use. By choosing to focus on the problem, they averted this spend in favor of something more viable.

Addressing the broader company just a few weeks later, Hockey shared the team's invalidation of the original idea as a win. "Folks approached us after hearing that story and said, 'Wow, you really told the CEO that this was a bad idea?' It seems to be changing how people think about sharing findings like that," cofounder Matt recalled.

John Hart, the Opportunity Area team's executive sponsor during the work, shared why this was so important to the company's growth, "We absolutely see this as a critical element in creating the environment to do meaningful innovation."

Cofounder Sarah agreed, "We know that we have a culture that is willing to take a risk. But actually experiencing it on this scale was really cool."

CUSTOMER RESEARCH: ASKING VS. OBSERVING

The shift from TAM to TAP is transformative for three reasons:

1. It steers our focus away from our own problems ("We want to gain share!") and toward the customer's problems ("They want to get from point A to point B as safely, quickly, and seamlessly as possible").

2. It shifts our attention from what exists today (corporate-owned assets like hotels and rental cars) to what could exist in the future (the sharing economy enabled by Airbnb and Lyft).

3. It relies not on what customers say they want (access to organic produce), but on what they actually do (buy more affordable, often inorganic produce). In other words, it reveals the commercial truth.

The classic marketing adage to give customers "what they want, when they want it, in the form they want it in" is exasperating when your focus is on new problems or needs; customers may not yet know what they want, when they want it, or what form they want it in.

Old-school tools like Voice of Customer research encourage customers to give feedback within the framework of what they already know. That is, when asked about a problem or need, they often reverse-engineer ideas based on current solutions. And when asked direct questions about their preferences and behaviors, they're socialized to project who they want to be and to tell us what *we* want to hear.

So instead of putting our faith in Voice of Customer research and other similar tools born out of the TAM mind-set, we must learn to observe what customers do and extrapolate how their behaviors reveal new opportunities. And no, we don't need to haul out the Magic 8-Ball to pull this off. We've simply got to think like entrepreneurs and do the legwork ourselves: Get out of the building and interact with customers, watch them in action, and draw our own conclusions. The evidence we're looking for is behavior. Discovery of new problems and needs lives in the realm of active, unreported, authentic customer choices.

We enter that realm by sending teams out to interview two populations:

PEOPLE WHO ARE ALREADY USING A GIVEN KIND OF PRODUCT OR SERVICE IN AN ATTEMPT TO SOLVE THEIR PROBLEM: We speak with them about where, when, why, and how often they use it. We ask why they choose it over similar solutions. We ask all the typical consumer research questions, then push beyond them into contextual information. We ask how the solution makes them feel, what it reminds them of, and what positive and negative associations the solution conjures.

PEOPLE SUFFERING THE SAME PROBLEM BUT WHO ARE DEFINITELY *NOT* USING THAT SAME PRODUCT OR SERVICE: These folks provide a vital counterpoint to the existing user base. We want to know what they're avoiding or pushing back against by not using this solution. We ask what about it turns them off, how does it make them feel, and what are they doing or using instead.

Here's an example: Say you make candy bars, but realize that people are starting to see processed sugar as Public Enemy Number One and want to explore alternatives for your company. As you consider a new TAP to address, you begin the research process. You talk to candy fanatics, candy store owners, specialty candy makers. But you also talk to Blue Zone diet folks who haven't had sugar in ten years, and really try to understand what needs, problems, and behaviors they're displaying.

As you speak with more and more people, your OA starts coming into focus. You learn that both die-hard fans and occasional consumers alike associate eating candy bars with "treating themselves" to something. Which allows you to focus on a new subset of questions: What triggers the urge to treat yourself? Is it accentuating a positive, or overcoming a negative? When do people treat themselves? How often? How does doing it make them feel? And you circle back with the outliers, too: What does somebody on a sugar-free diet do when they're feeling a little peckish and don't need to satiate hunger but want to treat themselves?

You're not in the sugar-peddling business anymore; you're in the "treat yourself" business. Which blows the doors off the candy factory and brings you out into a whole new world of ways to "treat" your potential customers. Depending on how bold you want to be, you could end up launching a new business unit that manufactures delicious yet healthful carob-based snacks; you could buy a small cosmetics firm that is gaining a fan base for their inexpensive yet lush lipsticks; or you could open a chain of retail stores that sell affordable succulent plants, perfect for that impulse purchase and sure to deliver a burst of clean air and brighter mood to any room.

This study and observation process will lead you directly to uncover previously untapped OAs, new worlds yet to be explored and conquered. But before you plunge into the jungle, torch ablaze, you'll want to evaluate if these OAs are worth your time, energy, and resources.

CALCULATING AND SIZING OPPORTUNITY AREAS

Determining how much money can be made from a market that does not yet exist is . . . tricky. With no measurable variables or existing statistics, attaching an earnings estimate to a bleeding-edge innovation can feel like guesswork. And honestly, some of it is. But we can ensure it's educated guesswork. (Remember, this is how VCs work day in and day out. They calculate the size of bleeding-edge opportunities as part of their due diligence of an investment, and we've incorporated their best tools into the Growth OS.)

> What is the goal of calculating TAP? To get a plausible understanding of how big an opportunity *could* be. Not to get an accurate understanding of what it *currently is*.

When we first started, Bionic used to tell our partners, "Don't even think about Total Addressable Market anymore! It's Total Addressable Problem only from here on in." But we got some vigorous pushback, especially when it came to sizing. Sinking time, money, personnel, research, and development into a market that could be minuscule is just plain foolish. You need some yardstick to measure how large and lucrative it *could* be, at least in theory. And so we've circled back to our old friend TAM. While TAM should not be the launchpad for new business ideas, it's valuable as a reference point for sizing OAs and TAP.

There are three back-of-the-envelope calculations to make when sizing up an OA:

1. Calculate the size of the existing market where people are using proxy solutions to solve their problem

2. Estimate the number of people who *need* to solve this problem if a radically better solution were available (and roughly what they might spend on that solution)

3. Estimate the number of people who would *want* to solve this problem if a radically better solution were available (and roughly what they might spend on that solution)

The first calculation is the TAM. The second is the "low end" or conservative size of the TAP, while the third is the "high end" or optimistic size of the TAP.

In the case of mobile phones, the TAM was the amount of money lawyers and physicians were spending on answering services and pagers so they could always be reached while on the go. The conservative TAP would include all professionals who would like to be able to communicate when they were away from their desks (multiplied by the amount they would be willing to spend for mobile access). The optimistic TAP grows to include literally anyone who speaks, even before they can type.

Ask yourself, "What do I know about the market today?" Then, "How big is the problem I want to solve?" Look at your answers in tandem, and think in terms of *orders of magnitude*. Is it 10x, 100x, or 1,000x bigger?

Current market knowledge can be helpful, but not in isolation. NYU finance professor Aswath Damodaran can attest to this: In a now famous exchange, he wrote a 2014 blog post saying that, based on the existing global taxi and livery market of roughly $100 billion, rideshare company Uber was overvaluing itself by a factor of 25.[1] (His analysis assumed Uber could command 10 percent of the fragmented global market for a TAM of $10 billion.) Bill Gurley, an Uber investor and board member, responded by saying, "In choosing to use the historical size of the taxi and limousine market,

Damodaran is making an implicit assumption that the future will look quite like the past. In other words, the arrival of a product or service like Uber will have zero impact on the overall market size of the car-for-hire transportation market."[2] Just three years later, Uber reported 2017 gross bookings of $37 billion. Uber and Lyft triumphed by recognizing that the current solutions addressing the problem were inadequate, and by creating a solution that directly addressed shortfalls, the TAP was larger than the TAM.

It can be intimidating to calculate TAP under the assumption that your solution will create a new market or explode the current one, but we need to do it anyway. We need to allow ourselves to contemplate the likely, the possible, and the extraordinary all at once if we want to enable the creation of revolutionary solutions.

THE STARTUP ECOSYSTEM IS MORE THAN JUST ENTREPRENEURS

We've spent this chapter digging into the approach that entrepreneurs and investors use to evaluate opportunities. The startup ecosystem is more than just entrepreneurs; it's also made up of angel and venture capital investors, and they all think this way.

Everyone embracing the Growth OS will need to shift from TAM to TAP mind-set. But how they apply it will vary. In the enterprise New to Big machine, the role of entrepreneur will be played by employees, while the investor role is filled by executive leadership. And the latter group's job isn't just handing out money. Both groups must be prepared to think and work in new ways, through different mind-sets of their own, ultimately challenging themselves to become *ambidextrous leaders*: operators in the core as well as creators of new growth.

That first step toward becoming an ambidextrous leader? Setting the permissions and boundaries for their entrepreneurial teams to work differently. Giving them permission to be wrong. Permission to question established wisdom. Permission to disrupt core businesses. Permission to run experiments and invalidate assumptions and move fast. Permission to behave like a startup even while they're embedded in a mammoth, hundred-year-old enterprise.

It sounds crazy, but it can be done.

4

THE GROWTH LEADER CHALLENGE

CHANGE IS HARD. IT'S ESPECIALLY HARD IF WHAT you're already doing has been even marginally rewarding and successful. This is why corporate leaders sometimes give us a little side-eye when we insist that they start thinking like venture capitalists. After all, money is being made, stockholders are mostly happy, nothing is technically broken. Are radical changes *really* necessary?

They are. They absolutely are. To capitalize on the startup ecosystem, you have to embrace all aspects of it, not just the ones that feel easy or comfortable. (Not that *any* of them are cakewalks.) And that includes training managers and leaders to support New to Big efforts by focusing on customer problems, celebrating productive failure, and relentlessly pursuing the commercial truth.

Let us share an example of this fundamental about-face: meet George Oliver.

In September 2017 George R. Oliver was appointed chairman and CEO of multinational conglomerate Johnson Controls. Prior to the 2016 merger of Johnson Controls and fire protection and security company Tyco International, Oliver had spent ten years at Tyco, including the last six as CEO. And before leading Tyco, Oliver had a twenty-year career with GE, where he served in operational roles of increasing responsibility across several divisions. To say Oliver is a phenomenal operator is as much of an understatement as saying Simone Biles is good at somersaults.

Bionic started working with Tyco in 2015 when Oliver and his team were searching for new ways to grow their business footprint. As they mapped out their strategy for the future they wanted to know what they could learn from Silicon Valley—to understand what made some startups so successful.

"We had a hundred years of success developing products for the fire and security industry, developing solutions, and then ultimately completing the traditional service on those installed systems, but we weren't thinking beyond," according to Oliver.

By now, you should be able to diagnose that situation easily enough: they were thinking TAM, not TAP. But, as it turns out, the root cause was one level deeper than that: Tyco was locked into a classic Big to Bigger mind-set.

"Let's face it, when you're a strong operator, you think you have all the answers, because you've lived through all the problems," Oliver continued. "So you're quick to provide the answer. We realized very quickly that a lot of that behavior was getting in the way of growth."

Since leaders *become* leaders by spending decades learning and observing and analyzing and achieving, they have a wealth of institutional knowledge and business acumen. Often, they also have a tough time accepting that, in order to install and deploy a growth operating system, they need to chuck much of that hard-won wisdom in favor of a handful of radical mind-set shifts.

"The challenge is that you're working with extremely intelligent people who've been highly successful by doing things in a certain way," agrees Debby Hopkins, the former chief innovation officer of Citi. "That's hard, because now you're saying it's not good enough anymore."

In the twentieth century, success meant becoming a global leader. But to be an enterprise CXO in the twenty-first century, you'll need to become *a growth leader*. What does that mean?

"Leadership today has got to be multidimensional. You've got to have strong operating skills. You've got to build strong teams. But you've also got to have a growth acumen that is ultimately the catalyst to long-term success," Oliver insists.

To foster New to Big growth you must learn how to become an operator *and* a creator. You have to become ambidextrous. Having worked with, interviewed, employed, and actually been new business creators ourselves, we've identified ten key mind-sets that transform operators into creators:

1. Turn Outside In
2. Focus on Do vs. Say
3. Embrace Productive Failure
4. Expire Your Data
5. End Your Addiction to Being Right
6. Lead Bullets Only
7. Don't Love Things to Death
8. Build Ladders to the Moon
9. No Success Theater
10. Become an Ambidextrous Leader

Let's go through them one at a time.

1. Turn Outside In

Most enterprises overvalue their own knowledge, expertise, and insight and undervalue the experiences, trends, and secrets that exist outside their walls. Yet the majority of startup success stories are driven by forces outside the entrepreneurs' control. VCs understand this.

We regularly ask VCs what percentage of their successes are due to market timing, luck, fate, whatever you want to call it. Their answers are always sky-high. "I think that being in the right place at the right time is sort of 99 percent of everything," says Albert Wenger, managing partner at Union Square Ventures. *Right, and on time.* We couldn't agree more.

VCs know that the real drivers behind their huge wins are external—changing regulations, the diminishing cost of a technology, consumer trends. It's not about them; it's about something *outside* of them, something happening on its own timeline and out of their control. Which means looking at the world from the inside out is a terrible strategy for creating something new. You have to Turn Outside In.

Starting with an R&D technology and searching for a customer to sell it to? That's inside out. Buying a company because they're threatening your market share? Inside out. Searching for a new channel for your existing widgets? Inside out. (And incremental.)

Outside In means asking, "What outside forces are happening to us? How is the landscape changing? What new enablers allow us to solve this customer problem exponentially better than it's being solved now? And how can we leverage our organization's unique capabilities, our 'proprietary gifts,' to capture and leverage this force?" As leaders, we need to be keenly aware of new and emerging market forces so that we can develop extraordinary ideas internally, and release them at the ideal moment. We need to see potential, and position ourselves to pounce when the time comes.

Here's an example of Outside In thinking in practice:

Unmanned aerial vehicles (more commonly known as drones) are a fantastic example of a technology that has gained traction on an unpredictable timeline. They were first used in combat in the early 1970s, but it took another forty years for them to become a regular tool of warfare. Once the technology was cheaper and more widely available, corporations began to consider how they might leverage it. However, early attempts at commercial drone use in 2012 by taco delivery startup Tacoraptor were quickly shut down by the Federal Aviation Agency (FAA), which didn't bode well for broader adoption. Two years later, the FAA issued guidelines that outlawed all commercial use of drones—seemingly a public rebuttal to rumors that Amazon was developing a drone delivery network—yet granted gas company British Petroleum (BP) permission to use drones to inspect their infrastructure in remote parts of Alaska. The latter ruling created an opening for commercial drone use to become acceptable eventually. While regulators initially took a conservative approach, it's only a matter of time before the wave sweeps through.[1]

So when we started working with a large energy company in 2015, we weren't surprised to learn that they were paying close attention to commercial drones as they looked Outside In. Over the next two years, we helped them seed an OA with solution concepts that leveraged drones, plus one very valuable proprietary gift to solve a huge customer problem. (Sorry, we can't tell you what it is.) The question they continue to ask as they run experiments to validate those solutions is *When?* When will the regulations shift and unleash widespread adoption of this technology? They know the time is coming, they're just waiting for it to arrive.

By turning Outside In, that energy company has created a portfolio of bets to ensure they are *right and on time* when it comes to drones.

Incremental Leaders

- Believe the potential success of a new product or business is wholly under their control.
- Have solidly established views of "how the market works."
- Look at competitive startups and think, "They're too niche."
- Believe being "on time" is when a customer starts asking for a solution, rather than demonstrating they need it through new behavior.

Growth Leaders

- Embrace the philosophy that they must be right, *and on time*, which means riding an outside force that is out of their control.
- Build a personal "advisory board" to keep them up to speed on relevant trends and technologies.
- Assemble a team to work on potential white spaces that leverage nascent technologies or trends that could reach a tipping point in three to seven years.
- Focus on how technology is growing or changing a market, or enabling a new customer behavior, remembering that the current market size might look different in a year.

2. Focus on Do vs. Say

Experienced marketers know that customers frequently have no idea what they want until it's placed in front of them. There's a legendary (though factually dubious) quotation from Henry Ford that is often trotted out at this point: "If I had asked people what they wanted, they would have said faster horses."

But venture capital investor Eric Paley insists that this attitude points to a level of arrogance and dismissiveness toward your consumer. "Good product managers don't ask their customers what they would like. It's not the customer's job to know. Instead product managers ask, 'Why would you like a faster horse? What do you want from a faster horse? Would you prefer your horse needed to eat less often, to stop less often? Would you prefer if it couldn't throw a shoe?'" The insight from this tall tale is that you actually need to ask the questions that uncover the root of the customer need.

Of course, back in the day, the alternative to polling customers was risky and expensive: to set up a factory, build a car, and hope people would both want it and buy it. You had to be a visionary, be right, be on time, and have gobs of capital to fund your experiment. Today, Ford could take a much cheaper and faster approach: do customer interviews as Paley demonstrates; size the TAP to ensure the opportunity is big enough; build a landing page featuring a prototype Model T, demo video, and sign-up forms; buy some ads on Facebook and Google; and test consumer demand for a few thousand dollars and in the space of a couple of days.

In fact, this very model for gauging customer appetite is employed by Tesla. The company set up online preorders for its Model 3 car multiple years in advance of delivery. People were actually signing up to buy (and putting down a $1,000 deposit!) before Tesla had a functioning prototype.[2] That is powerful evidence of customer intent, of a target market saying, "Not only can I actively voice my desire to own this product, I'm willing to back up that desire with cold, hard cash."

Do vs. Say is a mind-set that emphasizes customer *behavior*, which reveals far more commercial truth than Voice of Customer

(VOC) research. It's not just that customers may not know what they want; it's also that in VOC research, customers have nothing at stake. Experiments need to be designed in such a way that they *cost* customers something, proving out the respondent's true level of interest and commitment. Consider these two hypothetical research scenarios:

SCENE 1: Does this widget solve your problem, X? *Yes.* Great! Do you think you would buy the widget? *Sure.* Which one would you be most likely to buy? *The blue one.* How much would you be willing to pay for the blue one? *Probably $25 to $30.* And how likely would you be to buy this when it hits stores? *Oh, I'll probably buy it. It really is a great product.*

Research finding: Probable purchase of blue widget at price point of $25 to $30.

SCENE 2: Does this widget solve your problem, X? *Yes.* Great! Would you like to preorder this product right now? It costs $29.99, with free shipping. You can enter your credit card and shipping information right here, and you won't be charged until it ships. *Um, I mean, it's great, but I'm not sure I would order one right now.* Okay! No problem. Would you like to sign up for our mailing list so you can be the first to know when it is available? The mailing list will get first dibs when we launch. *Well, that sounds awesome, really it does, but I get so many emails, you know? I'd just rather not give you my email address today.*

Experiment result: Stated interest, but no conversion at $29.99 price point and no email signup. Value proposition not validated.

Two approaches to value proposition testing that yield two very different results.

Leaders need to model the Do vs. Say mind-set by urging their teams to design experiments that require an exchange of value, rather than rely on any research that is based on surface-level customer responses. When teams say that "we know" something, leaders must push them on *how* they know it. What experiments have they run to demonstrate that truth?

Incremental Leaders

- Lean hard on traditional research methods, such as Voice of Customer.
- Assume that consumers know what they want and that they can articulate it.
- Spend money on any and all projects that traditional customer research data predicts will succeed.
- Let VOC research drive product design.

Growth Leaders

- Validate or invalidate solutions based on customer actions.
- Design every experiment with an "ask." (There must be an exchange of value or it's research pretending to be an experiment.)
- Solicit feedback from customers in a way that allows them to answer in a completely unbiased manner. (Customers often tell you what they think you want to hear if they think they're being judged.)
- Create a testing environment with a range of experiment designs in order to use the right tool at the right time.

3. Embrace Productive Failure

More often than not, after one of my keynote speeches for an enterprise leadership team, a CEO will follow me backstage and, in a quiet voice, admit one of their deepest fears: that their company leaders don't tell them the truth. In those rare moments of vulnerability I will look them in the eye, take a breath, and with radical candor confirm, "They don't."

CEOs are shielded from the truth because their employees have been trained to live in fear of making mistakes, betting on the wrong horse, championing a concept that flops. Established companies aren't set up for failure, and executives aren't positioned to understand its value. So people tiptoe around leadership, or spout best-case scenarios about improbable outcomes rather than fess up to misfires and wrong turns.

Of course, the failure we're talking about isn't an irreversible blunder that leads to bankruptcies, legal action, catastrophic job losses, or putting people in harm's way. That, friends, is straight-up bad. No, what we're talking about are the cases when the *dream* doesn't line up with *reality*.

Like when everyone's sold on the dream that A will be the future of the company. The team already procured resources and mapped out a five-year road map for A, and they're eighteen months into the journey. Then they run experiments and learn that although customers don't want A, they're actually pretty psyched about B. From the outside, the obvious choice would be to update the vision, pivot to B, and get cranking on a new direction. But in an enterprise where unselling the dream is fraught with judgment, politics, and more, the cost of learning is too high. It's your entire career. So the whole company tacitly agrees to ignore the commercial truth and continue on with a project they all know will fail. We call those projects "zombies." They are the walking dead, and everyone knows it, but they suck up talent and resources because no one will kill them.

Embracing Productive Failure means lowering the cost and increasing the speed of learning. It means small, fast, and cheap failures that ultimately point you in the right direction rather than morphing into big, painful, and expensive failures (ahem, New Coke). It means leaders who create an environment that can kill zombies, freeing up resources and attention for opportunities that are still alive. It means welcoming the commercial truth even when it is counterintuitive, even when it requires a sharp pivot.

We may not always see it, but the legacy of productive failure is all around us: WD-40, the famed lubricant that silences squeaks and loosens stuck parts, got its name from the 40 tries it took to perfect the formulation.[3] Bubble Wrap was originally invented in an attempt to make trendy, textured wallpaper (an obvious failure); it only became an "overnight success" years later when IBM wrapped computer parts in it for transport. The first synthetic fabric dye was actually a failed attempt at making an artificial version of quinine, an antimalarial drug. The chemistry experiments created an oily sludge, which was terrible as a drug but turned silk a beautiful shade of purple.

At Citigroup, we worked with an internal team called D10X to build a startup ecosystem for the bank. Debby Hopkins, former CIO and founder of Citi Ventures, was already well aware that the key to this work could be increasing the speed of their learning. "It's not just that you're learning about yourself, you're learning about the process, you're learning about the technology. There's absolutely no substitute for experience."

Venrock partner and VC Nick Beim appreciates productive failures when funding a startup team: "For us, when someone's failed and they're really thoughtful about it, and they've gotten much smarter, they're going after the new opportunity armed with what they've learned. That can lead to terrific outcomes."

The entire entrepreneurship/VC ecosystem is based on a portfolio theory that assumes a high rate of failure. We'll dig deep into this concept in chapter 7, but for now, a quick overview: The data show that 60 percent of VC returns come from just 6 percent of capital deployed, while more than half of deals lose money. The top VC firms don't have fewer misses, just bigger hits.[4] Yes, this means even the very best VCs usually make investments that fail. Spectacularly. But they increase their odds for big wins by looking at potential opportunities through a lens of "What if this works?" rather than "What if this fails?"

Bringing this model into a healthy, discovery-driven, growth-obsessed established company means the company must be willing to try dozens of things, be comfortable with watching the majority fail, and be self-aware enough to extract wisdom from the process. A company that "fails to fail" is both missing out on learning opportunities and leaving money on the table. A leader who inhibits productive failure is inhibiting meaningful growth.

Venture capitalist Esther Dyson uses the phrase "Always make new mistakes!" in her email footer.[5] Great advice from a venerable investor. We must give our teams permission to fail, and create systems to ensure those failures are productive.

Incremental Leaders

- Fear all internal failure, associating it with lost time, money, and resources.
- Feed the zombies instead of pivoting.
- Are surprised when a "sure thing" bombs after years of planning.
- Struggle to get the full picture of why a project failed.

Growth Leaders

- Think of failure as an inevitable by-product of risk-taking and a necessary input for meaningful learning.
- Build a portfolio of bets knowing that many will not succeed. (Again, more in chapter 7!)
- Always ask if there is a cheaper/faster way to get to the same learning.
- Are honest and open about mistakes without being judgmental. Leaders discuss them in meetings, write about them in newsletters, and make their entire company comfortable with learning from failure.

4. Expire Your Data

At the risk of sounding like somebody's ornery granddad, business cycles sure do whizz by awfully fast these days. Want proof? Let's take a stroll through the acceleration of change over the past eleven thousand–odd years. (Don't worry, it'll only take a paragraph.)

When agriculture came on the scene around 10,000 BCE, workers were able to develop an enduring and reliable mental framework for how their world worked.[6] Once they'd determined the yield of corn from an acre of land and the demand for corn in the nearby market, they could execute on that knowledge for their entire working lives. The industrial revolution in the nineteenth century brought faster cycles, but it formed the core of the global economy for nearly two hundred years. Since most modern business careers span twenty to sixty years, that speed of change allowed most workers to spend a lifetime relying on the same time-tested techniques. Today, the commercial internet is only about thirty years old, closing in on the length of a single career cycle. And the mobile internet revolution is only ten years old, a mere fraction of a career.[7] Major cycles of change in technology and customer habits are happening more frequently as the years tick by.

Which means that business data remains relevant for significantly shorter periods. Just a few decades ago, we could successfully leverage heuristics, learnings, and data from the early phases in our careers for present-day decision-making. Now that change is moving at such a clip, we can't reliably do that anymore . . . but old habits die hard. Disregarding hard-won experience is unnatural to us, and it requires conscious effort to abandon earned knowledge.

At Bionic we set guardrails with our partners that only allow data from the last twelve months and forecasts up to three years into the future. Data more than a year old needs to be revalidated. And forecasting beyond three years is intellectually dishonest, because the technology and business models are unknowable beyond that horizon.

As an example, many of the business models that failed spectacularly during the dot-com boom, such as pet food delivery and online currencies, are now—twenty years on—the basis for profitable and sustainable businesses.[8] How did Chewy succeed where Pets.com failed? What was different?

Julie Wainwright, the former CEO of Pets.com, weighed in in a *Business Insider* article: "Here is what the world looked like in 2000: there were no plug-and-play solutions for ecommerce/warehouse management and customer service that could scale, which means that we had to employ 40+ engineers. Cloud computing did not exist, which means that we had to have a server farm and several IT people to ensure that the site did not go down. There were less than 250 million worldwide internet consumers in 2000. Now there are 5 billion."[9]

Expire Your Data means that instead of a knee-jerk reaction of "That doesn't work. Don't you remember what happened to X?" we should ask, "Why could this work now? What is true about the world today that could make it viable?" It means a business venture that was catastrophic ten years ago might be lucrative today. It also means that as leaders, we must constantly be questioning what is true about the market and our place within it.

Seasoned VC Albert Wenger agrees: "Break all of the rules. I think most great investments are great specifically because they broke some rule that you previously had." As a growth leader, it's your responsibility to encourage your teams to question and test the strongly held views and assumptions that support day-to-day business. "This is how we've always done it" is a death knell. Burn the rule book, expire the data, and look at the problem with fresh eyes.

Incremental Leaders

- Believe they can forecast markets, business models, and technologies multiple years into the future.
- Are embarrassed about the risk of making the same mistake twice.
- Are known for saying, "Been there, done that."
- Read the same books, attend the same conferences, and listen to the same thought leaders as they always have. (You might even say they're in a bit of a rut.)

Growth Leaders

- Examine and understand new market forces and technologies before pursuing a project.
- Put an expiration date on data, typically no more than twelve months in the past. Then they reset and revalidate all assumptions on any old data.
- Always ask, "Why now? What has changed and what's driving that change? How do we know and when did we learn it?"

- Are intellectually honest about what *should* work vs. *used to* work vs. *does* work.

5. End Your Addiction to Being Right

Nobody likes to be wrong. Seriously, even science says so: Psychologists have found that when we're "unfairly" accused of something, the cognitive dissonance we experience is jarring and deeply uncomfortable,[10] triggering the same areas in our brains that register physical pain.[11] Consultant and author Judith Glaser has compared our collective desire to be right and win arguments to an addiction, from a psychological perspective.[12]

Addiction or no, the constant need to be right is unproductive on several fronts. First and foremost, it turns us into intolerable jerks. Equally worth noting, bullheaded insistence that we're right is utterly ineffective in convincing the other party of our rightness. Cornell researchers found that, in the context of debate, language that is more hedged and open to alternatives is considerably more persuasive.[13] And in the longer term, clinging to the notion that we're already right can hold us back from *actually being right*. When we close ourselves off from discussion and experimentation, we miss out on discovery.

Andy Grove, one of Intel's founders and its legendary former CEO, had a useful approach to protect against this addiction in internal discussion: the mantra of "disagree and commit."[14] This philosophy allows team members to voice disagreement while simultaneously deferring to another team member and committing to make the chosen path work. Both sides recognize that nobody can really know the right direction with total certainty, so they move ahead together rather than wasting time in debate.

Grove is not alone in his belief that wrongness can be productive. Former leader of GE Culture and cofounder of GE FastWorks

Janice Semper has admitted, "We had a culture of being addicted to being right . . . we had a culture of perfection. We didn't know how to partner with our customers and see their problems from their perspective. We had to train our leaders to lead in a different way. We had to get them to ask questions in place of providing answers."[15]

Debby Hopkins also sees the danger in addiction to being right. She says, "It's that inherent thing of having been very successful and really believing that you created that business. The challenge now is to bring to those incredibly successful leaders the understanding that the equations that we've all depended on have been dissolved. The real thing, the underscore, is that predictability has disappeared."[16]

Leaders who jettison their addiction to being right often gain access to new worlds of inspiration and inventiveness. Part of implementing entrepreneurship and venture capital as forms of management within your company means encouraging venture teams and their advisors to be open to proving themselves wrong in order to unlock new opportunities.

Incremental Leaders

- Tell teams what to think, rather than asking questions about why they think A is the right decision or how they learned B.
- Highlight data in presentations that support the thesis being defended, while dismissing data that doesn't fit the narrative.
- See changing their minds as "flip-flopping."
- Value decisiveness over learning.

Growth Leaders

- Ask questions—real, open-ended questions (not leading ones)—rather than giving answers when teams share work in progress.

- Change their vocabulary: evidence that proves their point is not a "win," an assumption proved wrong is not a "loss." Both are learning.
- Make decisions based on the evidence the teams collect, even if it contradicts what they "know" is true.
- Reward the "truth tellers"—the individuals who are willing to contradict company wisdom, industry best practices, even their biases.

6. Lead Bullets Only

Reporters writing corporate profiles and academics writing business cases *love* their silver bullets. Nothing makes a story sing like a single brilliant feature or strategy that launches a company into the stratosphere or saves it from certain doom. Silver bullets are appealing because they're deceptively simple and seemingly effortless. "If we work hard enough and smart enough we'll discover the *one* thing that will solve our complex and seemingly intractable problem!" the argument goes. Not to be a downer here, but that is straight-up magical thinking.

In fact, the idiom derives from an ancient belief in the magical power of silver and the widespread folklore that silver bullets were the only way to kill werewolves or supernatural beings. (Talk about an intractable problem . . .)

Early in his career, entrepreneur and venture capitalist Ben Horowitz learned his lesson about silver bullets. While he was working as a product manager for web servers at Netscape, Microsoft released its Internet Information Server (IIS). Microsoft's product was five times faster than Netscape's and would be given away for free. Furiously, Horowitz planned a set of partnerships and acquisitions that he believed might shield Netscape's product from the attack, but when he outlined his plans to his engineering counterpart, he got an earful. His colleague, who'd gone toe-to-toe with Microsoft many times before, told him, "Our web server is five times slower. There is no silver bullet that's going to fix that. No, we are going to have to use a lot of lead bullets." So Horowitz and his team focused on a barrage of small improvements that collectively fixed the performance issues, and eventually Netscape beat Microsoft's performance benchmarks.[17]

Lead Bullets Only is a mind-set that acknowledges that when it comes to growth, there are no silver bullets. This work is hard, and it takes a lot of metaphorical lead bullets to install a growth operating system that seamlessly interfaces with the rest of the enterprise. There isn't one framework (or book, or conference, or thought leader) that will magically fix this. There is no way to "avoid the battle," as Horowitz puts it. You have to "go through the front door and deal with the big, ugly guy blocking it."

Ultimately, companies eager to grow must be willing to invest the resources, time, and political capital to develop a robust and integrated growth capability rather than flit between innovation "fixes" that are little more than flavors of the month. Leadership must be willing to acknowledge that this process is not about "solving the quarter" but about long-term survival.

Incremental Leaders

- Constantly search for "quick wins."
- Know the "lead bullet" solution, but avoid it because it's daunting.
- Are reactive to innovation rather than proactive.
- Believe acquiring a company or copying a competitor or *any one thing* will solve their problems.

Growth Leaders

- Take a hard look at their situation and consider all the levers they can pull and the opportunities for change. Remember it's never just *one thing*.
- Look at how they are measuring and rewarding work. Changing priorities requires updating metrics and incentives.
- Keep a dual timeline for success: looking at the arc of progress over months and years, while celebrating small wins and fast learning over days and weeks.
- Don't drink the Kool-Aid: PR is not reality, and those purported "overnight successes" were decades in the making. (Keep your eye on the prize.)

7. Don't Love Things to Death

We all remember Lennie from Steinbeck's *Of Mice and Men*, right? The big galoot who loved to pet soft animals, yet always ended up killing them? Lennie was not a malicious character, or a budding sociopath. He was well-meaning and brimming with affection for critters of all kinds—he just didn't know his own strength. He, quite literally, loved things to death. (That's right, we can be downright literary when we want to be.)

Shifting to a process that involves tons of trying and failing makes it tempting to hold fast to any successes, no matter how tenuous they may be. You've invested company time in dozens of small innovation bets, learned from the ones that didn't prosper, and provided more funding to those that did. It's only natural to latch onto any and all bets that show traction or promise.

Experienced entrepreneurs know that the first customer revenue is often the "wrong" revenue. Early adopters are typically not representative of your potential customer base, and it's unwise to draw broad conclusions from that initial small sample. Startups often spend months, or even years, working to understand who the "right" customer is, tinkering with pricing, loyalty, margins, and operations, before they are ready to scale. These are the "ugly teen-age years" of a startup, and you can't skip them. Otherwise, you're scaling something that is still unproven. (And that could mean a big, expensive failure, which is the *wrong* kind of failure.)

It's also tempting to coax success from bets by showering them with the best amenities established corporations can offer, like great infrastructure, privileged access to customers and partners, expensive staff, and special attention. As leaders, we want to reward progress and play to our strengths. But restraint fosters creativity, and comfortable entrepreneurs will never get as far as scrappy ones. In a study of award-winning work from 1.7 million people by employee incentives consultancy O.C. Tanner, researchers found that the most creative and successful outcomes were born from limitations and constraints, rather than unlimited resources and blank canvases.[18]

New to Big growth requires leveraging your expertise, talent, and strategic assets in innovative ventures, while also preserving a healthy and genuine entrepreneurial environment where startups must prove their models and earn their keep. Trust that, and don't force early promise forward too soon.

Incremental Leaders

- Jump the gun whenever a venture shows even a glimmer of potential, and push it to prematurely scale by showering it with extra resources ... and extra pressure.
- Measure success by increasing hype, not customers, growth, revenue, and, in time, profits.

- Have a team that isn't hungry enough.
- Believe the first customer revenue is representative of the entire customer base, and push teams to "get on with it" and replicate that success before they're ready.

Growth Leaders

- Before providing support, ask, "If this were a stand-alone startup, what resources would it have?"
- Search for team members who are gritty and thrive under limited constraints. These are less likely to be the "high-potential" employees and more likely to be the makers, tinkerers, and truth tellers.
- Practice restraint when a team/startup begins to take off. They don't absorb it into the core at the first sign of success; instead, they give it six to eighteen months to work through its "ugly teenage years" first.
- Encourage teams to push past the first customer revenue and search for the (profitable, obsessed, loyal) customers they need to scale the business.

8. Build Ladders to the Moon

In May 1961, President Kennedy gave a speech before a joint session of Congress announcing that the United States would land a man on the moon before the end of the decade. The first-ever "moonshot" was a huge and ambitious goal to accelerate our space technology and catch up with the Soviet Union, which had already launched a man into orbit earlier that year. On July 20, 1969, with just 164 days before the decade was up, *Apollo 11* landed on the moon and Neil Armstrong took his "giant leap for mankind."

More recently, the term *moonshot* became buzzy corporate speak when Alphabet's innovation arm—called simply X—described itself as "a moonshot factory." X has launched wildly ingenious projects such as Waymo self-driving cars and Loon balloons designed to make the internet globally accessible. Jealous? Understandable. The notion of a fully funded think tank that's allowed to ponder and experiment with truly transformative ideas is incredibly seductive. However, it's easy to forget that ideas are presented to the public in their most mature stage; we aren't privy to the step-by-step evolution that transformational ventures typically take.

A "moonshot" is usually framed as a big, expensive, risky bet, but that original "giant leap for mankind" took eight years of methodical research and development, which built on *decades* of quiet work before that. Each bit of progress, each increment of success is a rung in a ladder. Backstage activity is what makes audacious achievement truly possible, and we must invest both patience and resources into cultivating it. In other words, when businesses contemplate our own moonshots, we're far better served by building ladders than catapults.

Building a "ladder to the moon" may sound tedious and deeply unsexy, but here's why it works: It allows you to learn and capture competencies out of order when necessary. With a catapult, you put all your resources into constructing a device that offers one exhilarating chance to reach the exosphere. With a ladder, you start at the bottom, locking in your rungs as they come available, and do so even if rung nine shows up long before rung four. The ladder lets the learning process unfold organically, and even if it feels a little messy, it gives you a complete, intimate understanding of how you reached your goal. And it gives you the ability to cruise both up and down multiple times instead of putting all your energy into a single, colossal effort.

SpaceX, a commercial rocket company whose founder's ultimate ambition is to colonize Mars (so we guess that would be a "Marsshot"), has experienced out-of-order rung progression and the importance of the slow build. Here's a timeline of the company's progress:

2001: SpaceX took its first baby steps toward its lofty goal by exploring the use of cheap, third-party Russian rockets to send greenhouses to Mars. When the sourced rockets proved too expensive, the company decided to build its own.

2008: SpaceX launched its first spacecraft into orbit. (Note that seven years have gone by. Seven years, people!)

2010: Making commercial rocket flights financially feasible for non-billionaires meant recovering and reusing the spacecraft, so SpaceX focused on honing these protocols. The year 2010 saw the first recovery, but reuse was still a ways off.

2012: To make itself financially viable, SpaceX launched a side business as a space delivery service. This year saw its first delivery of a satellite to a space station.

2013: Next came delivery of supply shipments to space stations.

2015: SpaceX achieved its first controlled landings on land and on an ocean platform.

2016: The company began studying the viability of launching a network of four thousand satellites to provide global internet access. The profits from this operation would fund its interplanetary ambitions.[19]

2017: SpaceX saw its first successful reuse of a proprietary rocket. (A rung the company wanted in 2010, but didn't have until 2017.)

This stroll through SpaceX's history shows how moonshots may be the ultimate goal, but smart entrepreneurs start small and tackle them step-by-step. The company quickly abandoned the unrealistic notion of aiming for Mars right away, instead developing the competencies it needed to eventually reach it. This approach differs from the incrementalism of "sustaining innovation" because each step is more challenging than the previous one, even when they come out of sequence.

There's nothing wrong with aiming for the moon. Expecting to get there in one shot, however, will just lead to disappointment. Focus instead on step-by-step progress.

Incremental Leaders

- Focus on the size of the solution only, not the bigger problem it's solving, and often kill solutions that seem too small.
- Dream of the day after launch, rather than the smaller wins they can aim for this year.
- Plan for continuous, linear growth from launch to the moon as if it happens by momentum.
- Are more worried about how to scale a startup, rather than helping the right cofounders and advisors just get the work started.

Growth Leaders

- Solve the first few pieces of the problem right now. (Over time, those pieces build a ladder to the solution.)
- Focus on portfolios of bets rather than single catapult

shots. (With a portfolio, teams can leverage learnings from invalidated bets to get closer to a solution that works.)

- Are willing to learn "out of order" if that's what it takes to keep momentum going.
- Deal with scaling when it's time to scale.

9. No Success Theater

Nobody likes to fail, we get it. But do you know what is worse than failure? Failure masquerading as success. The term *success theater* was coined by Eric Ries in his book *The Lean Startup*. He defined it as the action of "making people think that you are successful, [using up] energy you could put into serving customers."[20] Success theater is usually accompanied by "vanity metrics," stats that look great but fail to fundamentally measure the health of the venture.

For instance, a startup website that has high traffic but low conversion might focus on traffic in reports and press outreach to present a pretty picture. As the saying goes, "What gets measured gets managed," so traffic then becomes the focus of the team and perhaps the investors and advisors supporting them. But if the more relevant metric for that specific business model's success is conversion, the startup will struggle.

This shouldn't be an altogether new concept for established companies. After all, the quarterly dance of optimizing financial ratios for Wall Street analysts could also be categorized as success theater. Slashing assets to artificially increase ROA when you haven't been able to boost returns? That's success theater in a nutshell. (It stings, but you know it's true.)

In the context of launching new businesses, success theater can be deadly. Most corporations are used to focusing on a few large and relatively safe projects. They're not familiar with the high-risk nature of startups, where it's normal for more than half to fail. Ideally, large companies become more comfortable with this over time, cultivating a portfolio of small bets that are ramped up as they demonstrate success. But if they only *pretend* to accept this alternate way of launching and supporting products, that make-believe will mask the rot but never deal with it. (Remember our discussion of zombie projects?)

No success theater means putting on your big-kid pants and being willing to both hear and deliver bad news. It means measuring what's really happening rather than sifting for the metrics that paint a positive picture. It increases trust on teams, because the only story told is one anchored in reality, rather than illusion and political maneuvering. And it means when you do stumble across "good news," you can trust that it is more than optics. Ending success theater ultimately frees up talent and funding for bets with the potential to *actually* succeed.

Incremental Leaders

- Focus on successful *aspects* of their bets, instead of looking at their performance holistically.
- Hide failure, because it's politically damaging.
- Shy away from the weaknesses in their business.
- Have two distinct points of view on the business: the true one and the one they present to others (including members of their team).

Growth Leaders

- Present performance metrics in the context of the bigger picture. They take the bad with the good.
- Dig into signals and metrics that indicate weakness in the idea. That's where they'll find the opportunities to improve.

- Focus on the success of the startup *in the market.*
  Hiccups and triumphs in the testing phases help teams
  learn, but to drive growth, the endeavor must make its
  mark in the real world.
- Don't personalize failures—or successes.

10. Be an Ambidextrous Leader

Every business faces a trade-off between creating new businesses and operating those that already exist. Historically, breaking new ground has been the responsibility of entrepreneurs and R&D departments, while managing the status quo has fallen to managers and executives. However, true growth leaders must train themselves to handle both, to become fully ambidextrous.

Way back in 1991, Stanford professor James March tried to tell us this. He published a paper titled "Exploration and Exploitation in Organizational Learning" in which he outlined the importance of leadership tactics that balance old with new. March posited that—given its greater uncertainty and longer time frame—exploration is always vulnerable to being deprioritized. Exploitation is the safe bet, while exploration is unnervingly risky. And when organizations train themselves to be rock stars at exploitation and rack up a long list of exploitation-based successes, exploration becomes less and less appealing. Companies can coast along, exploiting their existing products, services, and core competencies, for quite some time. A complete eradication of exploration, however, leads to stasis and decline.[21]

"The only way to have this type of flexibility is to build a culture that makes change totally expected and acceptable—that's what will make these instances less painful," says Facebook's VP of product, Fidji Simo. "You create this culture by putting people in charge of a problem, not a product; reinforcing again and again that you're all working in a market where assumptions change and that's okay; releasing products early to get initial feedback and adjusting accordingly. If you do all that, you create an organization that can absorb change—and that's vital."[22]

On the ground floor it makes sense to task your creators with discovering new opportunities while your operators focus on executing against existing plans; but at the leadership level, you must learn to do both.

The huge advantage that established companies have over startups is their ability to take New to Big and make it Big to Bigger. And the only way for that to happen is if leadership speaks both languages and creates the interface between the two capabilities. Shifting from analyzing a strategic plan in the morning to coaching a startup team in the afternoon requires a mental dexterity that only comes with practice. Becoming an ambidextrous leader is your biggest challenge in your search for growth.

Incremental Leaders

- Have isolated pockets of the company dedicated to creative discovery. Their oversight is separate, and they are not integrated with other departments.
- Focus on the success of the margins rather than the launch of new projects.
- Feel anxiety over the decline of a core profit stream, rather than excitement about new opportunities.
- Let cash pile up on the balance sheet or use it for share buybacks to boost stock prices, rather than invest it in growth opportunities.

Growth Leaders

- Explicitly include both business-operating and business-creating experiences in leadership job requirements, and incentivize accordingly.
- Craft professional development plans that build "creator" competencies alongside "operator" ones for their leadership pipeline.
- Build business-creating processes and staff into the organization, rather than setting them off to the side or shipping them off to Silicon Valley.
- Evaluate New to Big through growth mind-sets, rather than traditional efficiency mind-sets. They use the right tools for the work.

FROM THEORY TO PRACTICE

In the first section of this book, we've laid out a philosophy. We've introduced New to Big vs. Big to Bigger, examined the market forces that drove a wedge between enterprise and startups, explained the importance of shifting from TAM to TAP, and explored the mind-set shifts executives must make to become growth leaders. This section has been focused on *why*: why old methodologies won't work, and why you need to head in a new direction.

In the next section, we'll get into *how*. We'll begin to outline the steps you'll take and tactics you'll implement to install a growth operating system in your own organization.

Ready? Let's do this.

5

DISCOVER A BIG, UNMET CUSTOMER NEED

BEFORE WE CAN SOLVE A PROBLEM, WE NEED TO DEFINE it. We need to understand who grapples with it, how often, and how deeply it affects their lives. When we're designing a service or product on behalf of a specific group of people, studying their behaviors, use patterns, and daily frustrations nudges us toward the most potent solutions. So our first step of the Growth OS is to explore the issue we want to attack and the various technologies or enablers we could use to blow it out of the water. That's Discovery in a nutshell.

SHIFTING FROM PLANNING TO DISCOVERY MODE

Startups know that the correct place to start is *not* with an answer, but with a question: "What are the needs of unserved customers, and how can I meet them in a radically better way?" As we've insisted in previous chapters, we need to stop zooming in so tightly on what we can make and who might buy it, and zoom out instead to understand what people need. When we uncover a need that can be met differently using new technologies or enabling solutions, we've landed on an Opportunity Area (OA). It can feel counterintuitive and awkward to shift focus from our core competencies to the customer's unmet need, but it's a shift that reorients our companies toward authentic growth and productive creativity. If we want to launch an endeavor that has a snowball's chance in hell of succeeding, we must start with the headaches and obstacles that large populations wrangle on a daily basis.

Yet here's the rub: Technological innovation and adoption is moving faster than ever before. It took nearly five decades for the telephone to reach 50 percent of US households, but it took a mere five years for cell phones to accomplish the same penetration. Electricity didn't hit the 10 percent adoption rate until it'd been widely available for thirty years; tablet devices reached 10 percent adoption after just five years.[1] Inventors are creating devices, systems, and services that consumers didn't know they needed, yet once these innovations are introduced, they're embraced with wide-open arms. (And wallets.)

To the untrained eye, these market-creating innovations seem to come out of nowhere. Who saw the peer-to-peer business model coming? Or the blockchain? These concepts are so new and so divergent that they abjure comparison, and that makes them slightly terrifying. We can't plan against the unknown unknowns, nor predict how many units we'll sell, because no one's ever sold them before. But the way things are going, those unknown markets are exactly where we need to focus our energy, attention, and money.

The traditional MBA toolkit—TAM analysis, financial projections, customer segmentation, competitor analysis, even go-to-market strategies—these are all tools that thrive in a world that is known, a world where the near future roughly resembles the near past. But when you're building in a world where the markets, business models, and technologies of the future are rapidly changing, those tools are less effective. In this world, strategic business planning breaks down because the target is unknown; in this world, you must instead venture forward through a discovery framework.

HOW THE DISCOVERY PROCESS WORKS

Instead of starting with a solution—something we want to build that we're (irrationally) confident is going to take over some market—the Discovery process begins with a question. More precisely, it begins with a question *about a group of people*. That question is, For some given group of people, focused on some particular aspect of their lives, what is top-of-mind for them? What are the problems they are trying hardest to solve, what unmet needs do they have, and how are they attempting to meet them currently?

Asking these questions without assuming we know the answers allows us to understand the problems that are truly important to our desired audience. For example, what needs do workers in the gig economy have that are invisible to companies who offer financial products to traditional, full-time workers? This in turn leads us to what we call "good hunting grounds"—areas where we can hunt for businesses to launch that will solve huge pain points, and where we have a real chance of creating radically new solutions to unmet needs. To continue our example, how might we meet short-term liquidity needs for freelancers and gig workers who have less predictability in their incomes than salaried workers?

The Discovery process can be simplified as follows:

1. Assemble a small, designated team
2. Pick a group of potential customers, listen, and observe

3. Consider relevant new enablers that could serve their needs

4. Understand the current and emerging business landscape, technology road map, and startup/venture ecosystem

5. Combine all of these inputs to identify OAs

6. Consider sizing, timing, and fit of each OA to downselect and arrive at the prioritized OAs—the hunting grounds—where we want to launch new businesses

Let's step through each of those in more detail.

1. Assemble a small, designated team

Discovery work should be led by someone who has the ability to see beyond what the company is already doing and envision what it *could be* doing. This may be a contrarian, someone who is eternally playing devil's advocate, or a person with a vivid imagination and the courage to pursue out-of-left-field ideas. The Discovery Lead also needs to have the position and credibility to take that contrarian view when facing down the CEO. Typically, this role is filled by an executive who is obsessed about the future of the company.

The people working alongside the Discovery Lead should be three or four folks who show a love of deep questioning and unbridled creativity. It will likely include a financial analyst who can help with market sizing, perhaps someone from your corporate venture capital team who has an eye on startup trends and VC investment flows. You might consider a technology expert from R&D, a madscientist type who's five years ahead of the technology curve, as well as a customer insights expert with ethnography skills. Consider the realm you're entering and the scope of your exploration, make a wish list of roles or personalities who could be beneficial, then fill those slots.

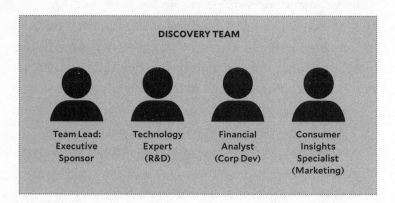

The Discovery process we outline here usually takes ten to twelve weeks. At the end of this process, you may find members of the Discovery team are good fits for other roles in the New to Big machine. Or they may transition back to their day jobs, yet remain available as advisors or additional resources for the startup teams. In either case, their contribution to the operating system cannot be overstated. Their mandate is largely to uncover and synthesize areas of opportunity for the company, creating a foundation of knowledge that will guide leadership to define their investment thesis.

2. Pick a group of potential customers, listen, and observe

Discovery work starts with people, but not *all* people, of course. In order to maintain a reasonable scope of work, we need to determine which demographic or psychographic groups or subcultures have big needs that we believe we can solve in radically new ways. The groups we define remain fairly broad—senior citizens, young mothers, millennials living at home, active single men—but bring some focus to how and where we'll conduct our initial Discovery research.

Our interest is in identifying pain points, but—as we hammered home in chapters 3 and 4—we never ask about them directly. Instead, we observe people in the wild. What we do with these subjects isn't proprietary or groundbreaking; much of it is drawn from ethnography, a hands-on, fieldwork-based research method common in the practice of anthropology and sociology.

Our Discovery teams typically start the work with members of segments that demonstrate extreme behaviors to understand a range of needs. (Think back to the candy bar example from chapter 3, where we mentioned talking to candy store owners *and* people who hadn't eaten sugar in decades.) These folks are of particular interest because they either have acute pain points, or they are solving common problems in novel ways. In the latter case, we're often able to improve upon the makeshift solutions they've created in order to serve a larger population. Focusing on the extreme cases helps us consider radical new solutions.[2]

Then the team will shift to subjects from the broader group, setting up in-home, at-work, or ride-along research moments. For example, instead of asking subjects about their frustrations around a pain point like meal planning and grocery shopping, we look in their fridges and pantries, ask what they cooked for dinner each night this week, find out if they go to the nearby farmers' market, and watch them pack lunches for their kids. We want to learn about their daily life and understand the values and beliefs that drive their behaviors. Then we want to dig into the subtext to suss out the core of their need.

For example, working with a company in the packaged-food space, we focused on mothers, studying their shopping, cooking, snacking, food storage, and restaurant-going habits, among other factors. We looked at their use of prepackaged meal kits, and discovered that although mothers loved the convenience, those with husbands and teenage sons reported that the men in their lives wanted larger portions. So the mothers bought supplementary food, cooked larger portions, found themselves gaining weight, and watched their cholesterol levels climb. Based on this information and a handful of other insights, observation showed us that for these women, nourishing their families was a higher priority than eating healthy themselves. That's not a phrase they would have used verbatim, but it's an inference we felt confident making based on our experience in their homes.

In doing this work, it's imperative to interview people within a given segment from multiple parts of the country to ensure you're getting a full spectrum of views and cultural nuances. Keep the groups small, observe and listen, then extrapolate what you see bubbling up. Identify things you see and hear multiple times and home in on the problems and needs those findings reflect.

3. Consider relevant enablers

Next we shift the conversation toward devising innovative ways to solve the identified problem. The Discovery process focuses on utilizing relevant enablers—trends, technologies, or business models—that can be brought to bear on a solution. How might a global financial institution leverage crowdfunding in a radically new way? How might blockchain smart contracts be deployed in a distributed supply chain to ensure transparency and document ethical and sustainable practices?

Most of the problems that people have are age-old problems. How do I nourish my body? How do I look my best? How do I communicate with my loved ones? New enablers have a shot at introducing a substantially better solution to these problems than existing solutions have in the past.

So in 2019, we set our sights on enablers like vertical farming, artificial intelligence (AI), 3-D printing, blockchain, virtual reality, drones, universal internet access, microbiome research, gene editing, and more. All the stuff that showed up in sci-fi films in the 1990s and is now, miraculously, available to the general public. Plus, we consider business models that are new or new to the company: peer-to-peer, direct-to-consumer, B2B, vertical integration, and more.

We want the Discovery teams to concentrate on technologies and business models that could plausibly be brought to bear on the problems of our target audience, but also remain fiercely imaginative about everything on the table. For instance, if a fashion brand wants to deliver a personalized customer experience, the company might say, "AI couldn't possibly help us with this. There's no way we're putting robots into customer-facing roles!" But AI encompasses things like speech recognition, sentiment analysis, and chat bots, which could have applications in e-commerce and in-store experiences. As we consider enablers, we want to keep our minds as open as possible so that we can see all the myriad possibilities.

Although we begin to dance around *how* these enablers might solve a problem at this stage, we spend most of our energy identifying and analyzing them. We generally end up with three lists:

1. Enablers and business models that *could be used* to address this specific issue

2. Enablers and business models that our competitors are *already using* to address this issue

3. Enablers and business models that are wicked cool but *totally useless* for this application

Out of context, many of these enablers seem thrilling but somewhat outlandish to the companies we partner with. The use of 3-D printing and drones? Maybe for a Philip K. Dick novel, but for an energy company or beverage producer? And yet when we do our homework, we learn that dozens of funded startups are already using 3-D printing or drones to bring solutions to market. Reality and fantasy are in lockstep. The enablers in group 3—the ones that are cool but useless—are discarded, of course, but many more end up in groups 1 and 2.

As our teams explore enablers, we are careful not to replicate market-dominating or crowded spaces. We'd never say, "Hey, let's look at mobile phone apps to solve transportation needs!" because at this point, that's been done to death. So if we're devising transportation-related solutions, we'll look at what's starting to emerge *right now*.

4. Understand the ecosystems

Neither pain points nor enablers exist in a vacuum. Once our internal teams have identified both, our next task is to consider everything that's influencing the target market, from new players in a field to emerging trends to unexpected partnerships. We take a few giant steps back from the work we've done so far and scope out all the relevant activity we can see. Considering this spread helps us form a thesis as to how the industry is changing and compile a macro view of the market landscape.

By putting both players and events on the board and considering how they've interacted in recent months and years, we begin to see trajectories and patterns. We see what's been done, what's been overlooked, and what's failed miserably. For instance, we've seen over and over again that while companies tout 3-D printing as the future of personalization, it has not delivered mass personalization at scale. (It is, however, incredibly useful in speeding up product development and creating flexibility in manufacturing systems.[3]) We see relevant trends in adjacent industries. We see ideas that should've succeeded but didn't . . . and if we're lucky, we see why.

Understanding the ecosystem is essential both because it educates us on all of the forces at work, and because it helps us understand timing. (Remember, we need to be right and on time.) A 50,000-foot view allows us to predict when world-changing enablers and shifts in behavior will collide, and to make sure we're there when the collision occurs.

Let's take a quick side trip to Hollywood for an example. For decades, film producers and movie studios have insisted that movies marketed to African Americans with predominantly black casts won't be profitable.[4] You're almost certainly aware that 2018 saw the release of Marvel's *Black Panther*, a film with a predominantly black cast, which became the highest-earning Marvel Cinematic Universe movie and had the fifth-largest opening weekend of all time.[5]

It can't be denied that *Black Panther*'s success is due, in part, to timing. In the last decade, new, global platforms have emerged that have been wielded to promote inclusivity, diversity, and a wide variety of social justice issues, and as such, representation of minority groups has seen explosive growth in popular culture, though much work remains.

And beyond social media, racial struggles and injustices have been widely portrayed in television shows, movies, music, and the news. Police shootings and harassment, the public reemergence of white supremacist groups, the continuation of mass incarceration, and hundreds of other aggressions, both macro and micro, are no longer hidden in the shadows. Activist groups, such as Black Lives Matter, have earned high levels of coverage for their movements, and have helped to firmly situate issues of racial injustice in a national conversation. The social and political climate in the United

States, in 2018, would therefore be much more responsive and engaged with these oft-discussed topics than they would have been twenty years ago, or even five. The conversations had become common, and the energy high.

So when *Black Panther* opened during US Black History Month in 2018, moviegoers of many races and ethnic backgrounds were ready. The film's creators carefully selected artists and collaborators who would fuel conversation around the movie and some of its social justice themes, including prolific rapper Kendrick Lamar, an outspoken advocate for racial equality, who produced the soundtrack, and renowned production designer and Afro-futurist Hannah Beachler (you might remember her from Beyoncé's record-breaking *Lemonade*).

Of course, *Black Panther* was not the first superhero film that featured black heroes (see: *The Meteor Man*, *Blankman*, *Blade*, *X-Men*, and *Captain America*), but in the words of culture critic Carvell Wallace, in these previous superhero iterations, "the actor's blackness seemed somewhat incidental. 'Black Panther,' by contrast, is steeped very specifically and purposefully in its blackness."[6] Again, twenty years ago, such deliberate steeping might have been perceived by some audiences, or even film producers, as a fiscally irresponsible choice, but in the United States in 2018, it was both financially and ethically impactful.

Timing isn't *everything* (remember, you have to be right *and* on time), but *Black Panther*'s record-breaking performance illustrates that timing can transform a great idea into a certified hit.

Ecosystem exploration has proven absolutely indispensable to the companies that Bionic has partnered with. While exploring the market landscape with one of our packaged-food partners, we got a clear picture of just how diverse and varied the company's competition really was. We noticed that Google—a company that played infrequently in the nutrition sphere—was incredibly bullish on a future food outlook that relied heavily on plant-based and synthetic meat proteins. Other than Blue Bottle Coffee, Google had steered clear of most food and beverage investments during its twenty-three-plus-year history. Yet in 2015, Google Ventures began investing heavily in Soylent and Impossible Foods, among other protein-pioneering companies.[7] When we began our ecosystem exploration with the partner, we were focusing mainly on the obvious Fortune 500 rivals in the packaged-food space. Our research forced us to broaden scope.

With this data in hand, we realized that our partner needn't be nearly as concerned with what its usual rivals were up to; instead, they needed to start keeping tabs on the Big Five tech companies. Our ecosystem explorations proved that the traditional competitive landscape had shifted dramatically in just a few years.

5. Plot the Discovery Grid

When we first discussed Opportunity Areas (OAs) back in chapter 3, we touched on the idea of positioning our companies at the intersection of consumer needs and enabling solutions. This step in the Discovery process is where we bust out the dry-erase markers and draw out a grid that plots those intersections.

The grid exercise is designed to help us get an even clearer picture of the overall ecosystem, and also shine a spotlight on untapped OAs. Here's how we do it:

- All potential enabling technologies are plotted on the x axis.
- All issues that are top of mind for our target population are plotted on the y axis.

- If a competitor company has addressed an issue from the *y* axis using an enabler from the *x* axis, that company's name is written at their intersection.

- If *no one* has addressed an issue from the *y* axis using an enabler from the *x* axis, the blank square at their intersection represents a nice, ripe OA.

SAMPLE DISCOVERY GRID

PARTNER: MAJOR AIRLINE
SEGMENT: BUSINESSPEOPLE

ENABLERS

PROBLEMS & NEEDS		BLOCKCHAIN	VIRTUAL REALITY/ AUGMENTED REALITY (VR/AR)	ARTIFICIAL INTELLIGENCE (AI)
	Touch base F2F with managers and/or employees			
	Meet colleagues to conduct business		Meta* ($50M funding/ $300M valuation)	
	Close sales deals			
	Scope out competition			
	Visit a partner's site			

PROBLEMS & NEEDS: Discovered by asking businesspeople *why* they use an airline's services—what problems are they trying to solve; what needs are they trying to meet?

ENABLERS: What are new tools that we can use to address those needs/problems?

*META: Startup focused on augmented reality headsets for next-gen "teleconferencing"

So simple, yet so fundamentally effective. Having done your research before plotting this grid, you've looked into your competitors' mistakes, you know how much money everyone is getting from investors, and you have a sense of how much revenue everyone's raking in. And with all that information plotted out in this format, you begin to see where the action is, where the heat is. You can see where the long-standing players have been, where new money is, where other VCs are investing. And perhaps most important, you can see the white space where nobody has thought to put their money.

Those blank spaces remain blank either because there's no real opportunity at the intersection, or because there's an opportunity there that no one has spotted yet. In the latter case, our team has identified a valuable OA and defined our "good hunting grounds." We've determined where to focus our energy and resources by mapping out pioneering solutions to real-world problems that haven't yet been tried by anyone else. And spaces where there is quite a bit of action would be a clear no-go zone for startups with limited resources and no infrastructure, but large organizations may still consider a play if they think they can use their scale and stature to win; it merely requires a different approach.

Honestly, taking in the completed grid and pondering those blank spaces is a pretty magical experience. All the ethnographic research, the brainstorming, the investigations of emerging technologies, the digging into competitor ventures, the metaphorical blood, sweat, and tears of the Discovery process gels into this gorgeous grid that can be used to chart a map of our business's future. We can see where there's a ton of action right now, where there are hints of action, where there'll be loads of action in five years, and where there's no action at all.

Even more profoundly, the grid doesn't just tell us where and when to build businesses. If a problem on the grid has no new enablers, it tells us where to direct our company's R&D money. If a problem is already being solved ably by someone else, it tells us to consider buying their company. Instead of just directing the development of new business endeavors, the grid creates a decision tree that seeds a full-fledged growth thesis within a company. It's designed to spark organic business (in-house startups), but also allows us to identify inorganic business opportunities (partnership and acquisition targets) and direct R&D resources; it helps us determine how to attack a problem comprehensively from multiple, informed angles. All that from one simple, hand-drawn grid! These are just some of the decisions the Growth Board will make as they make strategic and investment decisions across their growth portfolios (more in chapter 7).

6. Consider sizing, timing, and fit of each OA

In order to downselect and create some boundaries for our potential hunting grounds, our last Discovery step is to dig into issues of sizing, timing, and fit for each of our OA candidates. At its heart, Discovery is really about scoping work for the next team to fully explore, and these final steps help us to ensure that our scope is both reasonable and feasible. This is the part where we stand back, consider the various OAs that have made the rough cut, and decide which ones are worth pursuing.

Making those calls is equal parts art and science.

We start with sizing, since we want to dispense with any OAs that don't have the potential for massive impact and continued profit. When exploring a fundamentally new product or offering, Andreessen Horowitz's Benedict Evans suggests contemplating two key questions: "First, you have to look past what it is now, and see how much better and cheaper it might become. Second, you need to think about who would buy it now, and who else would buy it once it is better and cheaper, and how it might be used."[8]

The Discovery team does this by studying proxy markets, exploring how similar or related products are viewed, used, and consumed. This is simpler for some OAs than others, of course. Say we were interested in exploring self-driving cars. We have data galore on car-purchasing habits, and although autonomous vehicles are quite new, they're close enough to traditional cars that we can mine existing data and make reasonable predictions. Drones, on the other hand, have few logical proxies. In the past, if you wanted an aerial photo, you needed a helicopter . . . but far more people can afford camera-equipped mass-market drones than to rent choppers for the afternoon.

We may examine adjacent markets, too, if proxies are frustratingly hard to come by. And knowing that some of our proxies may end up being off-base, we explore a variety, harvest all the information we possibly can, and triangulate our sizing guesses. Then we move on to timing.

Our first timing question is always "Are there any blockers out there that would make pursuing this OA right now substantially more difficult?" The most common blocker is governmental regulation, either in terms of laws that prevent something from happening (like those that prevented Amazon from implementing drone-based delivery) or laws that need to be in place to protect our proposed venture (like pending patents or stronger copyright enforcement).

Our second question is "Why now?" We assume that a dozen entrepreneurs exactly like us, or smarter than us, have tried similar ventures and failed. So if we're going to chase that opportunity ourselves, we need to know how the world, the market, and our own capabilities have changed. Those who tried before were just as smart as we are, or even smarter, they had all the resources, and they still failed. So what factor, technology, enabler, law, or consumer appetite is present now that was absent when they attempted it?

Bionic recently teamed up with a partner who offered oral health products and was looking to leverage "internet-enabled interactivity" somehow. (No, we don't know what that means in the context of oral care, either.) After working through most of the Discovery process with their team, we pressed them to consider going in a different direction; we said, "Interactivity is simultaneously vague and restrictive. What about a lightning-fast toothbrush? Wouldn't people be ecstatic over a device that reduced the time it takes to brush your teeth from two minutes to ten seconds?"

Our timing research, however, proved that building such a

device is not possible. Not yet. The technology simply hasn't been developed to support those functions, and likely won't be available for another decade. So we had to reroute our thinking and pursue another path.

Timing is about zooming out and taking a real systems view of the space and asking ourselves, "Does this make sense now and is this the right time?" As corny as it sounds, we're looking to see if the stars have aligned, or if they'll lock into the right spots anytime soon, if they haven't yet. The whole Bionic team has watched businesses launch at the wrong time and fail spectacularly, and then seen someone come along just a few years later with the same idea and knock it out of the park. (Remember the Chewy and Pets.com example from chapter 3?)

Finally, we take a look at fit: "Is this OA a good fit for the company's core competencies, aligned with its mission, and in a space that appeals?"

To be clear, our current strengths shouldn't be our sole focus. We need to look beyond our core competencies when considering fit. To truly innovate, we must see beyond what we do well now, and imagine what we could do well in new spaces with the same skill set. Or imagine how building *new* core competencies could complement our existing ones.

You've heard of Airbnb, but have you learned to surf with a local in Costa Rica?

Before Airbnb was Airbnb, it was two roommates in San Francisco who struggled to pay their rent. A design conference was coming to San Francisco, and they thought that if they set up three air mattresses on their floor, they could charge a small fee to designers for a bed and the promise of breakfast. Three guests arrived, each paid eighty dollars, and the roommates knew that they were onto something.

After the conference in August 2008, Joe Gebbia and Brian

Chesky reconnected with their third roommate from college, Nathan Blecharczyk, and built out a website.[9] Air Bed and Breakfast launched for the first time as a roommate matching service, not one for room rentals.[10] But Roommates.com was already a behemoth in the space and quickly crushed them. They returned to their original model and relaunched. No one cared. They launched a third time at SXSW in 2008, but despite more than ten thousand conference attendees, they only had two customers (and one was Chesky).[11]

They decided to pitch investors anyway. Out of fifteen investor introductions from mutual friends, seven ignored the intro and eight flat-out rejected them. By this point, they were broke and in massive debt.

Then the Democratic National Convention came to Denver, and with traditional hotels unable to accommodate the massive influx of visitors, Gebbia, Chesky, and Blecharczyk found dozens of homeowners who wanted to earn a few extra bucks by hosting attendees. Traction was up, but the site still wasn't turning a profit. To make extra money, the founders redesigned cereal boxes into "Obama Os" and "Cap'n McCains" and sold them on the streets by the convention for $40 each.[12] In just a few days, they raised $30,000 in bootstrap funding.

Venture capitalist Paul Graham finally took notice. He invited them to Y Combinator, an accelerator that propels young startups into the market in exchange for a small stake in the company. But getting into Y Combinator didn't mean that the company was set. Fred Wilson of Union Square Ventures, along with many other investors, famously rejected them, saying, "We couldn't wrap our heads around air mattresses on the living room floors as the next hotel room and did not chase the deal. Others saw the amazing team that we saw, funded them, and the rest is history."[13]

And, to some degree, it is. The team dropped the lengthy name and switched to "Airbnb." The cofounders personally stayed in all the hosts' homes in New York City and reviewed each of them. When listings in New York were lower than in other cities, the trio rented a $5,000 camera and personally photographed dozens of homes, resulting in two to three times more local bookings and twice as much revenue from the city alone.[14] They soon picked up a check from Sequoia Capital for over half a million dollars. Within four years, Airbnb had launched in eighty-nine countries and hosted over a million overnight stays.[15] After seven funding rounds, investors such as Y Combinator, Sequoia Capital, Andreessen Horowitz, Founders Fund, TPG Growth, and Keith Rabois brought investment totals to over $776.4 million, and in the spring of 2014, the platform had a valuation of $10 billion, catapulting Airbnb to a higher valuation than Wyndham or Hyatt.[16]

But, of course, Airbnb hasn't limited their scope to housing rentals. A company founded on air mattresses and homemade breakfasts has grown to include an "events, experiences, and tours" site, too.[17] Users can learn karate or surfing, practice another language, explore Rome with a local, or even volunteer for service work. For its age, the Experiences tab of Airbnb grew *thirteen times faster* than the homes section had.[18] Experience hosts started earning thousands of dollars every year, with some hosts totaling $200,000.[19]

Though Airbnb started as a place to rest one's head at night, the goal has become "to be the one-stop shop for travel."[20] Every decision that the company now makes pushes them toward that status. While investors couldn't envision a world in which anyone paid to sleep on a low-end air mattress, and while few foresaw Airbnb's core functions to one day include all the experiences that accompany travel, Airbnb is becoming synonymous with all-inclusive traveling. In just nine years, with over 5 million listings in 81,000 cities and 191 countries, coordinating 300 million+ stays, and earning over $2.5 billion in revenue, their vision was clearly validated.

The reason we examine sizing, timing, and fit—and one of the reasons why the entire Discovery process is so crucial—is that the next step in the Growth OS involves dedicating a team to exploring the most promising OAs. If you're going to assign a team to work on a project full-time for several months, you need to make sure the endeavor has the potential to be the right size, being explored at plausibly the right time, and has the potential to work for your company. When you don't rigorously analyze and downselect all three of these factors, you could go down one of these common dead-end paths:

YOU GIVE THE TEAM A WIDE-OPEN SCOPE AND THEY DROWN: You say, "Explore millennials! Or China! Or AI!" And your team has no idea where to start, or what they're supposed to glean from any experimentation, and they make zero headway.

YOU GIVE THE TEAM AN OVERLY NARROW SCOPE AND THEY FREEZE: You say, "Go launch a fantasy sports app for millennials who are on track to become high-earners!" Tasked with this highly specific undertaking, your team is likely to start engaging in bad behaviors like surfacing only the evidence that supports the undertaking (success theater!), rather than listening to the commercial truth. They do this because the implication when you give them a super narrow scope is not "Explore multiple solutions to this problem," it's "Go execute on this project."

A primary goal of Discovery is to frame the opportunity and size it as accurately as possible. You want to scope out the hunting ground carefully so your team feels confident it can take action against it, but also isn't afraid to come back to you with truths that might invalidate it.

WHY BOTHER WITH DISCOVERY?

It's possible that some of you are saying, "Well, that sounds like commonsense research to me. Why would anyone launch a business without going through all those carefully calculated steps?" While perhaps others are thinking, "You've got to be kidding. That's going to take forever! Can't we just fast-track the research and skip to launch?" The hard truth is that Discovery does take time, and resources, and careful, thorough analysis.

When you perform traditional research then plow ahead, you may get lucky and hit on a solid solution for an enduring problem. But if something goes haywire along the way, you may not have the information you need to course-correct. And if your solution goes to market and succeeds initially, then tanks, you may not know why.

On the other hand, when you invest in understanding your potential market, researching new enablers, and forcing yourself to see the entire ecosystem, you can build your new bets from a place of informed, synoptic wisdom. You don't just know what to do, you know that it hasn't been tried before and that it will have a massive impact on a specific customer base. You may be diving into the deep end, but you're doing it with oxygen tanks and wet suits at the ready.

Now that we've identified our Opportunity Areas, it's time to validate our findings.

6

VALIDATE LIKE AN ENTREPRENEUR

A T THE SEED STAGE OF ANY STARTUP STORY, WHETHER cofounders are mapping out their new venture on a whiteboard or a diner napkin, they start by making four key assumptions: that there is a *cohesive* group of people, whom they can find, that shares a *common problem*; that their solution *actually solves* that problem; and that the business model for the solution is *viable* for the customer. Every successful entrepreneur knows that until those four assumptions are proven true, it would be useless to grow the venture. They'd be wandering in the dark, while their already-slim chances for success steadily diminish.

But most enterprise new-venture stories tend to skip this seed stage; they usually start by simply deciding to build something, making a big bet on a solution to a problem that has yet to be validated. Then they commingle making with commercializing, and any learning along the way that might disrupt the go-to-market timeline is ignored. In this environment, the truth is secondary to delivering on plan.

This chapter outlines the part of the operating system where the Opportunity Areas (OAs) we've discovered are transformed into portfolios of startups through a methodology we call Validation. By definition, to validate is to prove the legitimacy of something. It's as simple as that. In the startup ecosystem that drives New to Big, Validation is the practice of entrepreneurship adapted for the enterprise. It is the process of proving the "commercial truth" of a potential startup *before* making a large investment to formally launch and scale the business.

We're here to help you back up and start at the beginning. We want to demystify the methods, mechanics, and tools of entrepreneurship so you can learn at the speed and cost that startups do. Because, as they say, whoever learns the fastest, wins.

THE PRINCIPLES OF VALIDATION

At its core, Validation is the formalized methodology of entrepreneurship adapted for established companies. In formalizing this approach, we drew upon elements of Eric Ries's Lean Startup approach, Stanford d.school's Design Thinking, and Steve Blank's Business Model Canvas to create a repeatable process that helps us refine startups in the earliest stages through experiment-based learning. Ultimately, this approach increases the speed of learning and decreases the cost.

ASSEMBLING AN OA TEAM

Let's first define who is doing the Validation work: The employees you assemble for each OA are essentially your in-house entrepreneurs. Because they can come from many levels within the company and yet will serve as one cohesive team, we like to call them cofounders. While one may have been a manager in their previous role and another an associate, here they are equals.

Rather than being tasked to a specific project, as OA cofounders they will be committed to solving a customer problem by validating (and invalidating) a large volume of ideas. Like entrepreneurs in the startup world, these cofounders must thrive on ambiguity, love to tinker, and, together, bring a cross-functional set of skills along with the humility to do any job, large or small, to improve their chance of success. (In chapter 8, we'll dig into how to identify and select the employees who will thrive as cofounders.) Unlike the startup world, however, these cofounders will be tasked with exploring multiple solutions within an OA through a diverse range of experiments before downselecting to a single startup.

At the seed stage, OA teams are small and nimble, usually with three full-time cofounders:

- **COMMERCIAL:** One cofounder should be a strong communicator with deep business development, sales, and/or marketing experience, who is well-connected within the organization. For example, we've often seen former brand managers excel in this role. Think of this as your "startup CEO."
- **TECHNICAL:** One cofounder should be a Sherlock-level problem-solver driven by a desire to understand how things work. This person is analytically minded with strong business model or product experience. Depending on what field you're in, this could be a software developer, R&D scientist, or even someone with underwriting or risk management experience. This is your "maker."

- **INSIGHTS:** One cofounder should be connected
  to customers and motivated by the desire to truly
  understand their behaviors, motivations, and needs.
  For example, this could be someone from the marketing
  function, like a consumer insights associate. This is your
  "customer whisperer."

Guiding the cofounders is an Executive Sponsor for the OA, who serves to push cofounder thinking, ensure the rigor of Validation, and remove roadblocks. (We'll talk more about the role of the Exec Sponsor in chapter 7 when we discuss the venture capital side of the Growth OS, embodied by the Growth Board.)

CONSTRUCTING A GOOD HYPOTHESIS

Every startup begins with a set of hypotheses about the customer, their problem, the proposed solution, and the business model. In order to validate (or invalidate) that hypothesis, we have to start by identifying the assumptions embedded in it. Otherwise, we risk forging ahead without first confirming the legitimacy of that all-important problem-solution-market trifecta. A good hypothesis is made of assumptions that are simple and focused, each conveying one important idea that is directly related to the solution and the business model. Here's an example:

Let's say the customer need we are considering is American millennials who have pets with health concerns. One initial startup idea is that this demographic might be interested in a Fitbit-for-Fido type of product that helps them monitor their pets' health on a daily basis. This would be helpful both for pets with preexisting conditions (diabetes, kidney issues), and elder pets who are entering their twilight years. As we consider our hypothesis, we refine our assumptions:

TOO BROAD: American pet-owning millennials care about their pets' health.

(We can prove this quite easily, but it doesn't give us enough information to create a targeted offering.)

TOO NARROW: American pet-owning millennials will spend $150 on a device that monitors and reports on their pets' activity, heart rate, and sleep.

(Whoa there! A price point, product functions, and the specific data it will generate? Too much, too soon!)

JUST RIGHT: American pet-owning millennials are actively monitoring their pets' health.

(Simple, focused, actionable. "Actively monitoring" is behavior that we can observe, while "caring" is not.)

From this starting point, we can design experiments to validate that this population is, in fact, dealing with this need. If we learn that it's not, we can synthesize the experiment results to decide how to pivot: Is it the wrong customer? Or does this "need" not actually exist? Or are customers just not interested in solving this need? By starting Validation work with a hypothesis containing well-defined assumptions, cofounders set themselves up to raise these kinds of productive questions at every turn of events.

TESTING THE HYPOTHESIS

As we move from calibrating our hypothesis to testing it through experiments, we need to watch our step. This is where it becomes easy to create false positives by asking potential customers to articulate their needs. Remember, what customers *say* may be wildly different from what they *do* in real life.

Part of that disconnect is that typical customer research doesn't cost customers anything, so social conditioning kicks in and they take the nicer path, telling us what (they think) we want to hear. But the other part of that disconnect is that customers may not be consciously aware of their problem, or be able to articulate desired solutions that don't yet exist. By designing experiments to suss out facts about actual behaviors, we're able to uncover insights about the core needs we are seeking to address rather than rely on their self-awareness or limitations of imagination.

THE SKINNY ON EXPERIMENTS

We've found that enterprises have a distinct bias toward surveys and, when it comes to respondents, they believe that more is better. Entrepreneurs, on the other hand, prefer to whip up quick-and-dirty experiments to run on a dozen or so people to learn and keep moving forward. The question is always, *What's the quickest, cheapest thing we can do to decrease risk and increase confidence that we're moving in the right direction?*

At Bionic, we have a library of validation experiments that we employ at different stages or to test different types of assumptions. Here are a few of our most commonly used customer experiments (B2B and industrial experiments obviously look different).

EARLIEST STAGE
CUSTOMER PROBLEM INTERVIEW/ETHNOGRAPHY:
You don't need a prototype, or even a hypothesis to perform these experiments. These are focused on listening to people, asking open-ended questions, and observing behavior to

uncover unmet needs. We outlined an example of an ethnographic interview in the Discovery chapter.

WHAT IT GETS YOU:

Ethnography helps you get beyond the obvious problem and uncover the latent need. It also helps you develop empathy for the customer as you walk a mile in their shoes.

EARLY PROTOTYPE

FLIERS/POP-UP:

These are tests that can be done with almost no physical prototyping of any kind—just print up some fliers with your idea on them, put them somewhere public, and see how many people take them. Alternatively, you can set up a pop-up shop to engage people in discussion around a hypothetical solution, using a prototype as a stand-in for a real product or solution. In both cases, the aim is to gauge people's reactions to something that looks real at very first glance, but is not.

WHAT IT GETS YOU:

An early prototype is a tool we build to transform an abstract concept into something concrete. A low-fidelity prototype doesn't need to be a precise representation of the final solution. Instead, it is a way to synthesize and further refine the solution concept, clarify thinking, align the team, and (crucially) get specific feedback from customers.

LATER-STAGE PROTOTYPE

LANDING PAGE TEST:

To perform this test, we create a Google account and launch an ad campaign using search engine marketing, rotating in different ad copy to test interest levels. So if we were looking at a foot care OA, we might test ads that target different aspects of foot health: "Do your feet ache?" alongside "Do your feet stink?" alongside "Are foot issues affecting your marathon performance?" The ones that spark the most interest help us decide which solutions to pursue.

THE WIZARD OF OZ TEST:

In this scenario, we build a semi-automated interface for customers on the front end, but do all the actual work manually on the back end ("Pay no attention to that man behind the curtain!"). The customer doesn't see how the fulfillment is being accomplished, only the interface and results. This allows us to validate the value proposition before we invest in building out complete solution functionality. For example, you may think a new startup is using a fancy algorithm to recommend the best clothes for your figure, but if it's a Wizard of Oz test, it's actually a person (likely a cofounder) pulling together looks by hand to see if you like the offering before they invest in the algorithm.

WHAT IT GETS YOU:

Later-stage prototypes are all about building a preponderance of evidence. Strong signals from early prototype testing are qualitative in nature, and they move us toward these later-stage experiments that are aimed at capturing more quantitative data.

PRE-LAUNCH

PRE-SALES:

With products that are fully baked and getting ready for launch, a pre-sales campaign is a great way to measure interest in a do-vs.-say way and gauge ultimate intent to buy. Create a fully functional site, direct traffic to it, and start taking orders on your product before it is built.

WHAT IT GETS YOU:

Handing over cold hard cash (or in this case, credit card details) is the best "do" signal there is!

LEARNING FROM THE EXPERIMENT

Bias is an unavoidable part of human nature. There are dozens of cognitive biases that impede our ability to make good decisions. We default to things we already "know" to be true based on personal experiences, our rosy recollection of the past, or our preference for things we recognize, among other biases.

The power of Validation rests in our willingness to acknowledge our biased assumptions, design experiments to test those assumptions, and, finally, learn from those experiments, even if they contradict our predictions. That learning is the commercial truth, and it points us toward the opportunities for real, validated growth.

THE THREE SEED STAGES OF VALIDATION

As one Bionic in-house entrepreneur put it, "Validation is like making bread. The dough rises, and you punch it down. Then it rises again, and you punch it down. And all the time you're making the idea stronger."

All that rising and punching ensures that our proposed startups aren't just amazing in our heads, but have a chance of succeeding in the real world, too. As we cycle through the stages of Validation, we're constantly synthesizing our results and iterating on our hypotheses. We're celebrating productive failure and updating our assumptions and turning the crank once again.

That recursive process takes place across three seed stages, each of which will emphasize a different aspect of our three-tiered question:

1. Who is the customer and what is their need?

2. Does our solution actually meet that need?

3. Is the business model we're envisioning for the solution a viable one?

We need answers to all three before we can move on to building and, eventually, scaling the business. But we *also* need to bear in mind that all three are inextricably connected. This means that as we progress, changes in one dimension will cause the other two to adjust accordingly. If our understanding of the customer problem shifts or expands, the solution and business model will change in tandem. If we're exploring the solution and hit a major snag, we must be prepared to go back and recalibrate our comprehension of the problem and also adjust our vision for the model.

As you might have gathered, this means that Validation won't progress in a nice, neat, linear way. There will be some zigzagging or spiraling in addition to what feels like clear, forward progress. Remember, though, that none of this means you're wrong or falling behind. This process creates an ongoing dialogue between the learnings at the solution level and the OA level. We may kill and pivot many solutions, and through that gain great clarity about the OA. Validation not only ensures you don't launch untested solutions, but also points out when you're not thinking about the right OA altogether. (This is why CFOs fall in love with Validation: It saves you a ton of money.)

With that caveat about the zigging and zagging out of the way, we decided to lay out the seed stages in a linear progression because we want to impart a clear understanding of all three. Before you can start building, you need to know what to build. And to know what to build, you need evidence validating your customer, their need, your proposed solution, and the best way to bring that solution to market.

Seed 1: Search for the root cause of the customer problem

The first seed stage is about uncovering deep insights into people and the root causes of their problems. The mantra for Seed 1 experimentation is "What are the results from our experiments telling us about the problems within the OA?" Throughout Seed 1, the team is constantly thinking about whether they're examining the right ideas and looking for the spark of insight that will lead them to a bigger opportunity.

What does this look like in practice?

A few years back, we worked with a partner who was interested in foot health and wellness, and as we worked our way through Discovery, we realized that this was a surprisingly large problem that encompasses many populations. Since your body interacts with the world from the ground up, changes in your feet change everything. Feet, like teeth, are a barometer for overall human health, and when they're achy or chapped or in pain, it affects everything from mood to mobility.

Foot health is also an issue that impacts different customer groups in different ways. A marathon runner may be concerned about corns or bone spurs; an elderly person might experience pain due to chapped or cracked skin; a woman in her thirties might find herself newly unable to tolerate high heels as the fat pads in the ball of her foot naturally deteriorate. Everyone's feet wear out or break down, but the causes of foot-centric issues are diverse.

So as we started Seed 1, we worked to identify which problems were acute enough that customers would seek and pay for a substantially better solution. Although we explored pro and amateur athletes as a potential target customer, our problem interviews and ethnographic research revealed that a large proportion of senior citizens were feeling this problem acutely *and* were likely to embrace new solutions. So we chose to focus there.

Now, this partner specialized in chemical engineering, so most bone- or joint-related issues were going to be tough for them to address. It made sense to consider concocting some creams or lotions, but we were aiming for markedly better, drastically different solutions from those currently stocked in the foot-care aisle at Walgreens. So we started kicking around the idea of partnering with a startup that was 3-D printing shoe inserts, and injecting the insoles themselves with various treatments: anti-sweat formulas, anti-chafe medications, or conditioning creams. Developing an understanding of the customer and their problem propelled us forward into Seed 2: solution validation.

VALIDATION FUNNEL, SEED 1

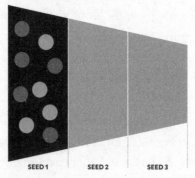

SEED 1   SEED 2   SEED 3

The purpose of Seed 1 experimentation is to validate:

- **WHETHER THERE IS A REAL PROBLEM:** In other words, do we have evidence there is a real need, or was this just a hunch?
- **WHETHER THERE IS A COHESIVE GROUP THAT FEELS THIS PROBLEM ACUTELY:** To launch a viable venture, we will need to consistently acquire customers. In order to do that, we must be able to identify *who* experiences this problem *acutely enough* to seek a solution.
- **HOW BIG THE TAP IS FOR THAT COHESIVE GROUP:** Although we looked at TAP when we first scoped the OA in Discovery, as we get more specific about the problem and learn more about which customers feel this problem, we gain more understanding of the size of the opportunity and whether it is large enough to proceed.

Seed 2: Putting solutions through their paces

Seed 2 is about ensuring we offer exponentially better solutions than whatever our customer is currently using (we call these "10x solutions," though ten times better is almost always a stretch goal). This stage is also often about acquiring our first customers who are part of a potential beachhead market: They're who we want to win over first, before bringing our offerings to the wider world. But now, instead of looking for insights into the root of their pain (which we tackled in Seed 1), we're devising experiments to reveal insights about our proposed solutions.

Experiments at this stage require slightly higher-fidelity prototypes than our last round, often a working Alpha. (When we make the leap from images to code or from sketches to a 3-D prototype, we create what's called an Alpha: something that works but with limited functionality. In the case of B2B or industrial businesses, an Alpha could take the form of a Letter of Intent or other on-paper expression of interest.)

Here's an example of Seed 2 experiments with a banking partner a few years back:

Our partner wanted to find ways to support freelance workers, many of whom weren't well served by traditional banking services and products. Big banks don't always offer credit cards or loans to folks who can't produce W-2 forms, and don't make their main offerings friendly to people who juggle multiple jobs and have fluctuating incomes. We all know that the gig economy is booming, but the banking industry hasn't done much to accommodate the shift.

One OA team put forth the hypothesis that "freelancers both want and lack freelancer-specific banking products, support, and tools." They ran it through Seed 1, and confirmed it was a real problem. When it passed into Seed 2, we homed in on the subproblem of fluctuating income and real-time gaps in cash flow or solvency, something that makes freelancers pull out their hair in large handfuls. Our proposed solution offered the 1099 crowd access to customized, short-term financial products based on their projected dry spells.

In addition to offering peace of mind during work droughts, the solution was also designed to provide truly accessible support. We streamlined the application process, built in pre-approvals, and made these financial products relatively hassle-free and easy to secure.

So what did all this look like in terms of actual experimentation and testing? Well, Seed 2 experiments can take a variety of forms, but in this case we worked with a dozen customers and had them interact with a variety of low-fi prototypes. We sketched out a possible app, and printed out the various components onto pieces of paper. (We said it was low-fi!) Then we walked them through the different screens, and took them down different paths through the app: "If you click this menu, here are the options you'll see. Where do you want to go next?" As they made choices, we took notes and asked questions.

Before we started coding and building an actual app or website, we wanted to understand what a freelancer might actually seek and use. If we mocked up five features, and all twelve of our customers completely ignored feature number three, we knew we should cut it.

We also asked them for qualitative feedback: "How does this live up to your expectations? You said you were really interested in an app that helps you anticipate income gaps. We made one; what did we do right, and what did we do wrong?"

Once we'd gotten a round of feedback on our printout-app, we created a prototype that was clickable but not fully active. About half the buttons didn't work, and it utilized static data, but gave more of an authentic app experience. And *then* we mocked up an actual app that would take in and process some of our testers' information but still wasn't fully functional. Our goal with these iterative prototypes was to continually ask our beachhead customers, "Is this solution living up to your expectations? Is it doing what you hoped it would do to solve your problem?"

VALIDATION FUNNEL, SEED 2

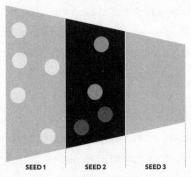

SEED 1   SEED 2   SEED 3

The purpose of Seed 2 experimentation is to validate:

- **WHETHER OUR INITIAL CUSTOMERS LOVE THE SOLUTION WE'VE OFFERED:** In other words, is there appetite for this offering?
- **WHICH KEY FEATURES EXCITE THEM MOST:** When we know what our customers need most from a solution, we can focus on that, which positions us to deliver significantly higher value than current solutions offer.
- **HOW WE WILL MEASURE THE EFFECTIVENESS OF OUR SOLUTION:** We need to have a clear picture of the metrics that matter, and easy ways to capture data about them.

THREE LENSES TO EXAMINE SOLUTIONS THROUGH

When I started writing *The Startup Playbook*, I had two burning questions for the veteran entrepreneurs I interviewed: How did they select their ideas? And what did they do in the first five years to keep their companies going and keep them from dying? What I discovered was that the founders' learnings could ultimately be distilled into five lenses through which they vetted and built solutions to customer problems. The first three lenses are vital to keep in mind as you work through Seed 2 Validation.

1. PROPRIETARY GIFTS

Every company that has achieved extraordinary success has something that sets it apart from the competition. This "something" could range from technical knowledge to deep industry experience to an asset or built-in operational advantage *that no one else has*; it's a proprietary gift unique to the organization that cannot be replicated. This gift creates an unfair advantage; the company that possesses it is specially equipped to tackle certain consumer needs efficiently, effectively, and in profoundly new ways. When you can identify your company's proprietary gifts and bring them to bear, you can change the world. When you boldly embrace your unfair advantage, you create your own shortcut to prosperity.

Proprietary Gifts in Action: In 1994, Amazon launched as an online bookstore, but founder Jeff Bezos's long-term vision for the company was considerably more ambitious. Over the next decade and under his guidance, Amazon established and refined its supply chain and distribution model first for books, then leveraged it to expand into CDs, software, video games, electronics, apparel, furniture, food, toys, jewelry, and more. As Amazon marched on into more and more categories, it systematically chipped away at the primary point of friction in e-commerce: waiting for your order to be delivered. Bezos had the foresight to predict that a company with a truly effective, robust fulfillment at its heart could be transformative. Rather than pursuing profitability, Amazon leaned hard on their proprietary gift and invested in building unmatchable fulfillment systems, distribution centers, and other delivery infrastructure. It set the standard for free two-day delivery with its Prime service, then shrunk the window further with same-day and (in certain areas) one-hour delivery. That proprietary gift has created a moat around Amazon's existing e-commerce business while also creating a competitive advantage as it builds new businesses like AmazonFresh alongside forays into the brick-and-mortar grocery business with the acquisition of Whole Foods.[1]

2. PAINKILLERS, NOT VITAMINS

Successful solutions solve a problem that is big, painful, and persistent: a repeated behavior or constant need that customers wrestle with on an ongoing basis. And the solution cannot be a vitamin, something that is nice to have and that you might even buy once, but that, on a day-to-day basis, probably sits unused at the back of a shelf. It must be a painkiller, something you ensure is always in stock and easily accessible because it solves your immediate need, effectively and consistently.

When the solutions we devise are painkillers for our customers' ailments, we can build entire companies around those solutions. And if we make ourselves totally irreplaceable, even when those customers think about quitting us, they won't. Even when they see shiny new solutions popping up, they won't walk away.

And on the flip side, if the customer problem isn't akin to chronic pain that needs soothing, we'll struggle to create a strong case for a successful solution.

Painkillers, Not Vitamins **in Action:** In 2015, Fitbit reported sales of 4.5 million devices with revenues up 235 percent from 2014.[2] But while the company was quick to tout device sales figures, they neglected to disclose that active daily users for the wristband were in decline. ("Success theater" in action! Focusing on impressive metrics instead of the most meaningful ones.) While many people were eager to buy a wearable device to track their health stats, about one-third of these owners ditched their device within six months. Additionally, there's no strong research that proves Fitbit is a key factor in weight loss and health management.[3] So, while Fitbit was a leader in sales of wearables, the device's overall effectiveness was more along the lines of a vitamin than a painkiller. It was a nice to have, but if you forgot to put it on one day, it wouldn't kill you.

In contrast, Nike recognized a recurring, deeply aggravating pain point for their customers and created a new business model around it. If you happen to be a parent, you've probably noticed that kids can wear a brand-new pair of shoes for approximately four days before growing out of them. Parents worldwide are in a constant state of shopping for shoes for their growing children (a singularly thankless task for many), and doing so feels like setting their money on fire. Enter Easy Kicks: Nike's subscription service that gives kiddo customers access to new shoes whenever they want 'em for $20 per month. The program is a logistically new way to engage with customers that both creates a recurring revenue stream for Nike and turns a painful experience into a peak experience for parents and kids.[4] People will never stop having kids, and kids will never stop growing out of their shoes, and parents will never stop resenting the endless buying cycle. All of which makes Easy Kicks an innovative and effective painkiller.

3. 10X IMPACT

When our companies have the means, talent, and desire to expand into new markets, narrowing the field of potential ideas can feel overwhelming. As we evaluate those ideas and decide which ones to abandon, we need to be ruthless. Ideas that produce incremental improvements are a waste of our time. We're searching for revolutionary, potent, dynamic ideas that will have significantly more impact than their predecessors. Ideas that create marked competitive differentiation. This isn't about chasing competition or relying on the typical benchmarks of success. This is about generating and nurturing ideas that have the potential to solve big, painful, unsolved problems while generating tens of millions of dollars in revenue (which can grow into billions).

***10x Impact* in Action:** When Sara Blakely launched Spanx in 2000, "girdles" had gone the way of the dodo and "shapewear" was not yet a thing. Yet she knew there was a gap in the market; since no other solutions were offered, women had been cutting the legs off their control-top pantyhose to get the upper half's figure-smoothing effects. This new customer behavior indicated a better solution would sell well. So she designed a sturdy Lycra undergarment that eradicated the bulges, bumps, and pantylines that plague women of all ages and sizes. Even the earliest iterations of Spanx were easily massively better than hacked-off hose, since they packed more shaping power, addressed more problem areas, and could be washed and worn multiple times. Once women got wind of this new foundation garment, Spanx began flying off department store shelves. And although plenty of knockoffs have since emerged, none have eclipsed the Spanx brand. Blakely created the shapewear market, and by building it on a product that was 10x better than the existing solutions, she was able to transform one idea into an undergarment empire.[5]

Seed 3: Honing the business model

Now that we've confirmed the customer problem and gotten a rough read on the proposed solution, we need to be sure there is a repeatable and scalable business model for the solution. In Seed 3, we're testing our proposed economic exchange of value, whether that is based on customer revenue, advertising revenue, or some other monetization opportunity. We're keeping an eye out for metrics and working to understand which handful of them actually matter for this business model. And we're looking ahead to determine which operational hurdles might be the most challenging as we move into building the startup.

To see this in action, let's take a trip to Mexico City.

We worked with a financial services company to help create some user-friendly, modern online banking solutions for its Mexico City customers. The city itself is forward-thinking and incredibly cosmopolitan, but somehow its banks have remained in the dark ages. Part of the problem is that many people in Mexico just don't trust banks. It's a very cash-rich society and also a very high-crime society, so people are wary of the bank-grade security required for checking their balances and transacting online. Instead, they go to physical branches and wait in line—usually for an hour or longer—to make deposits and handle their banking needs. Our partner wanted to launch a digital banking experience that Mexico City residents would truly trust to make investments, track daily spending, and monitor savings. The hypothesis was that a better online banking solution would help customers monitor their spending and save more intentionally.

Initial testing in Seed 1 and Seed 2 revealed that small business owners were particularly eager for a solution like this. Since they were often commingling their personal and business accounts, they saw real value in a tool that would help them keep careful track of their expenditures. We mocked up a banking app in Seed 2 that performed well in experiments, so the team moved into Seed 3 to validate the assumption that online banking customers would keep higher balances across accounts, which was how our partner earned money. This assumption was crucial to the success of the venture's business model, and it needed to be tested.

We ran a pilot in Mexico City with one hundred people, loading a rough cut of the banking app onto their phones and asking them to use it for ninety days while we monitored their behaviors. We also gave them a daily banking assignment, something like "Move money from account A to account B today," or "Pay a bill online." We studied their activities and watched carefully to see if being more informed as bank customers positively impacted their spending habits.

To our delight, it did! The small-business customers loved having the ability to monitor their cash flow more closely, and ended up keeping higher checking and savings account balances overall. The team's next step was to nudge them toward investing.

Typically, to get a money market account in Mexico City, a customer would have to go to a bank branch, do a ton of paperwork, and speak with a banker just to invest a couple hundred dollars. And each customer would have to do this *every time they wanted to invest*. Archaic, to say the least. So the team began working on ways to take the banker out of the equation and facilitate investing through the app.

We then gave the improved app to our same hundred-person sample, encouraged them to use it, and studied their behaviors. Sure enough, the lower barrier to invest via the app made them 80 percent more likely to invest money versus customers who were limited to a banker at a branch. Hard to argue with those numbers.

VALIDATION FUNNEL, SEED 3

SEED 1   SEED 2   SEED 3

The purpose of Seed 3 experimentation is to validate:

- **WHETHER WE HAVE A SCALABLE BUSINESS MODEL:**
  This involves acquiring customers and delighting them (in
  B2C models, this should be 100 to 500 customers; in B2B
  models it should be 1 to 3).

- **WHICH METRICS ARE MOST IMPORTANT TO THE
  BUSINESS MODEL:** For any given business, there could
  be dozens of trackable metrics. The focus at this stage
  should be to discover and begin to improve the three
  to five metrics that drive the core of your business. For
  example, for a particular e-commerce business, it could
  be variable production cost per unit, customer acquisition
  cost, inventory turnover ratio, cash conversion cycle, and
  production throughput time.

- **WHICH OPERATIONAL CONSIDERATIONS WILL BE
  THE MOST DIFFICULT:** Before we graduate from the
  seed stage into building and scaling, we need to have a
  read on which obstacles will be the most challenging as
  we build the startup. Are there operational hurdles like
  returns or fulfillment? Legal complexities like varying

laws across states? Or perhaps this startup will face regulatory challenges if you try to build it inside the enterprise (which might suggest it would be easier to spin it out as its own entity).

KEEP POUNDING THE DOUGH

Remember that Validation isn't a one-shot deal, nor is it linear. It's an iterative process to test ideas quickly and inexpensively and to reveal both flaws and strengths. It gives cofounders the tools to test the most critical assumptions they have about the customer's problem, the solution, and the business model. It ensures rigorous examination of biases and uncovers the commercial truth of a startup.

In this chapter, we laid it all out step-by-step, but in practice it's not so clean. Throughout Validation, teams shift their focus from problem to solution to business model to customers, revisiting assumptions across all three categories as they progress.

So if the process isn't linear, why bother separating one stage from another? Especially since that's not how it's done in the "real world."

Think about an eighteen-year-old high school graduate who wants to become a doctor. Before she can start writing prescriptions or even land a residency at a hospital, she's got to learn the building blocks: cells, biochemistry, physiology. In order to fix what's wrong with her patients, she needs to understand how they work from the inside out, and in great detail. At eighteen, she's got the drive and the talent, but she doesn't have the knowledge. She's a beginner. And only after she's polished off her undergraduate degree, four years of med school, and another three in residency and fellowship can she *legally and confidently* use that little rubber hammer to bonk your knees.

Similarly, all our partners are beginners when they first start

Validation. And beginners need structure, trustworthy procedures, and repetition. They need to watch the dough rise, then punch it down. Watch it rise again, then punch it down. All in the name of making the idea stronger.

When the idea has graduated from all three stages of seed, it's ready to head out into the world as a baby startup at the Series A stage. There's still no guarantee it will become your next $1 billion business, but by progressing through the seed stage and learning through cheap, fast, productive failure, you've eliminated or corrected the biggest errors in your original vision, and your odds for success continue to rise.

We've introduced the entrepreneurship side of the Growth OS; this is the part of management that determines what work to do and how. Now it's time to shift our focus and meet the venture capital side. Enterprise entrepreneurs cannot thrive on their own; they need investors to fund their work and champions to clear roadblocks and offer advice. We call this guiding body the Growth Board.

VALIDATION AT WORK IN A NONPROFIT: CHILDREN'S CANCER ASSOCIATION

Children's Cancer Association (CCA) is a nonprofit organization whose mission is to create transformative moments of joy for kids who are facing cancer and other serious illnesses and their families. All their programs are free of charge and focus on music, friendship, nature, and community support; everything that is important to healthy kids and their families, and become exponentially *more* important once they receive a serious diagnosis.

Founder Regina Ellis created CCA more than twenty-two years ago after her daughter Alexandra died of cancer when she was only five and a half years old. Regina set out to create a new organization that would position joy as best practice in pediatric health care environments across the nation. Bionic connected to CCA through a former partner of ours who is the organization's founding board chair. She believed that CCA, with its innovative tenets, would benefit from formalizing their methodologies and deepening their processes.

"As a purpose-driven organization, we have strong, entre-preneurial roots," says Ellis. "We run CCA more like a startup or business than a traditional nonprofit. Our partnership with Bionic was an extraordinary opportunity to strengthen our op-erating capabilities and embed a new innovation mind-set at a time of significant organizational growth."

The cross-functional CCA internal team decided to focus their efforts on teen patients. The organization's hospital partners had been consistently reporting that their teens were struggling, which just makes sense; teens experience serious illness in a specific and challenging way. They have a sense of their own mortality and they understand the gravity of a cancer diagnosis in a way that younger kids simply can't grasp. They're already coping with the emotional, hormonal, and behavioral health issues that come with being a healthy teenager; add a life-threatening diagnosis on top of that and the need for support and community becomes even more im-portant. Teens have also sometimes felt they were "too cool" or had outgrown CCA's core programs, which focus on music, mentoring, nature retreats, and family financial support. To challenge this, the organization chose to use Validation to craft a tailored program for teens.

THEY STARTED WITH TWO HYPOTHESES

1. Seriously ill teens have a need to connect with their peers on their own terms.
2. Seriously ill teens have a need for purposefulness, skill building, and learning.

PROPOSED SOLUTIONS INCLUDED

- Offering individual music lessons in the hospital (since teens are interested in skill building)
- Coordinating group music lessons (which have the potential to foster peer connection)
- Creating photography classes, makeup tutorials, craft workshops, or other skill-building instruction (for those who aren't interested in music)
- Organize a trip to an "escape the room" experience as a way to get out of the hospital environment (in case teens just want to be left alone to rest and recover while in the hospital itself)

SEED 1 TESTING

The CCA team posted flyers in the hospitals with sign-up sheets for the proposed teen programs, such as music lessons, photography, knitting, and makeup tutorials. They also went room to room and asked kids if they wanted to sign up, or if they wanted to just take a flier and think about it. Lastly, the team created a website where kids could sign up for programs as well.

The response? Deafening silence. They realized one of their core assumptions was that teens wanted to connect *on their own terms.* Yet their first round of experiments didn't test that assumption.

So CCA decided to solicit some direct input. They gave their teen patients the option to participate in what was basically a design-thinking workshop, a forum for offering suggestions on programs they actually wanted and needed. The hope was that attendees might have recommendations that could help shape the next round of proposed solutions.

SEED 2 TESTING

After that first meeting in November 2017, CCA realized that these forums could be the very solution that teens were hungry for: a way to connect with their peers. Co-creating programming might be a way for these young people to give back and feel a sense of purpose. These groups also helped the organization better understand the needs of kids who have dealt with extended hospital stays, serious illness, and an awareness of their potential mortality.

And so CCA's Young Adult Alliance was born. In March 2018, CCA hosted their second teen meeting, packed with icebreakers, brainstorming, the sharing of personal stories, advisory sessions on potential programs, and more. The attendees gave input on ideas generated by CCA staff, and also offered up ideas of their own.

SEED 3 AND BEYOND

Only now that they have a sense of the customer problem and solution is CCA considering the "business model," which in their case means raising third-party donations.

"Rather than going out and fund-raising and then spending a ton of money to launch a program that we haven't fully vetted or validated, the Validation process has helped and indeed required us to be more intentional," explains Abby Guyer, CCA's former vice president of brand.

CCA leadership believes the Growth OS has helped them take innovation out of the boardroom and embed it across the organization. They've started to see assumption-questioning and experimentation-focused thinking bubble up in meetings, even around day-to-day work. Employees at every level are asking themselves, *How do I articulate my assumption? Then, how do I test against it before I act, and certainly before I spend money against it?* As a nonprofit, CCA believes they have a responsibility to be good stewards of the money that donors entrust to them, and Validation helps them be sure they're testing before they invest.

"I think it would've been a missed learning opportunity if every experiment we conducted knocked it out of the park," Guyer told us. "Now we're learning how to stop focusing on our needs, not to take it personally if an idea doesn't resonate, and instead to really think about stakeholders and solutions. We're asking ourselves constantly, 'Is it a vitamin, or is it a painkiller?'"

We couldn't have said it better ourselves.

7

INVEST LIKE A VC

MOST PEOPLE INCORRECTLY ASSUME THAT DISRUP-tive ideas are the exclusive domain of startups, and that bigger, traditional organizations just lumber along refining their existing offerings. But plenty of long-standing companies employ talented intrapreneurs who dream up and hack together leading-edge ideas. The problem is that those creators frequently have no viable way to get their products into market.

They must first wring money out of budgets, which are allocated annually, so they'll have to wait until the next planning cycle. And then they'll have to compete for funding on an ROI basis, even though the ROI of their new idea is unknowable at this point. Then they'll have to pitch to their peers in the relevant business units, convince marketing to get on board, persuade or distract compliance, and cajole legal. If any of those folks push back, express doubt, or refuse to support an idea, it can die a slow and silent death before senior leadership even gets a whiff of it. And if their new idea competes with an existing moneymaker for the company (even if their solution is substantially better!), they literally don't stand a chance. No one in management is incentivized to disrupt the core.

Sure, you can probably think of a time when someone moved fast and did something big. Someone with lots of political capital, institutional knowledge, and a little bit of air cover can achieve something big . . . *once*. But they can't do it over and over, and neither can other people who may have the right idea but not the other skills to navigate all the red tape. The power to say yes to disruptive ideas resides at the top, while most everyone else is actively mitigating risk, because that is what they're being paid to do.

No, the problem isn't a lack of ideas. And it's not that the CEO and senior leaders aren't open to those ideas. The problem is the lack of a venue for those ideas to be heard directly by leadership, and the lack of permission for teams to pursue them.

This is where the Growth Board comes in.

OPERATE LIKE AN EXECUTIVE, CREATE LIKE A VC

Remember *waaaay* back in chapter 1 when we talked about the Growth OS as a dual-engine management machine, driven by both in-house entrepreneurs and in-house VCs? So far we've focused on the processes in-house entrepreneurs (Discovery team members and OA cofounders) use to identify and vet potential bets. Now we'll start looking at how those bets get approved, funded, and supported using an investment and decision-making group that we call the Growth Board.

The origin of our Growth Board model is one of those stories that could only happen by working and co-creating alongside our customers. It was early in my work at GE; Eric Ries and I were giving keynotes on the Lean Startup framework and the growth leader mind-sets, respectively, for the Oil & Gas division, which was led by CEO Lorenzo Simonelli. I finished my talk and had just taken a seat at a table in the back of the room when Simonelli joined me to ask a pressing question: "David, I've been thinking. I'm spending $700 million on over five hundred different programs, and I know they aren't all viable. How do I get half that money back? How do I get the teams to tell me the commercial truth?"

Without missing a beat, I realized the venture capital funding model of staged investments for startups along the seed/launch (Series A–B)/grow (Series C+) framework could apply to enterprise growth investments. The framework is one that requires teams to show evidence at each stage that is appropriate for the size of check they are requesting.

For the check-writers, this model allows them to invest small amounts when the risk is very high, and to continue investing in the work as the company shows progress. In essence, it derisks the venture. Rather than allocate the full funding for each project when it kicks off and have the teams take that funding for granted since it was "budgeted," this approach instills the kind of scrappiness and sense of urgency that startups face every day. It kills zombies—projects that deserve to be shut down yet continue to live on—and gives oxygen to the ideas that are commercially true.

As I finished sketching out this model on a piece of scrap

paper, Simonelli tore the drawing off the tablecloth and rushed it over to his leadership team, announcing, "Let's build this."

"We had a fundamental challenge in that funding allocation was done by engineering, and it was basically budgeted out each year based on the status quo," Simonelli told us recently. "There were a number of projects that had been going on for years and continued to be allocated millions of dollars even though they didn't really have an outcome in mind. So instead we brought the new product budgets down to zero and built them back from the ground up, reserving a quarter of the funds for the Growth Board to grant based on milestones."

He continued, "What it allowed us to do was stop things early on in the process if they didn't make sense. And we became more disciplined in the governance of capital allocation. It was a very difficult process to begin with because you have to move away from an entitlement mind-set. We found that, despite being really interesting, many of the projects weren't based on real assumptions."

Eric Gebhardt, the then chief technology officer of Oil & Gas, quickly became our partner in piloting the first iteration of Growth Boards. "As teams got on board, some of the biggest skeptics turned into some of the biggest zealots because they realized now that they could take on extra risk; they could go ahead and test bold hypotheses. I would say that we've always been very good at product development. This gave us the freedom to become great at it."

Three years after Simonelli installed a Growth Board at GE Oil & Gas, he asked his team to run the numbers on the speed and cost of new products introductions (NPIs) within the company. The number of days it took to introduce a new product had decreased by 70 percent over the cohort data from just three years prior, and the cost had decreased by over 80 percent. Bad ideas died quickly (and cheaply) while good ideas grew.

The recognition that startup tactics alone will never move the needle inside large enterprises—that startups need the funding mechanism of venture capital to balance out the growth ecosystem—was the crucial aha moment for me and my early Bionic collaborators, setting our young company on the path to build out the entire Growth OS.

The Growth Board is a body of senior leaders that typically includes the CEO, CFO, CMO, and other key executives. The Growth Board gives the teams building the startups the venue to be heard and funded, and to understand how their ideas might fit into the strategic objectives of the company. Members of the board act as internal venture capitalists, deciding how to allocate funding to early-stage ideas, consolidating learning from various initiatives, providing the permissions and boundaries within which the teams can create, and removing roadblocks when necessary. The focus of the board is to set growth goals, manage the portfolio of bets that are underway, and make investment and resource decisions to reach those goals.

This may be the point where you interject that you already have an investment committee in your organization. We totally understand how this may sound similar. But as you'll see, the Growth Board is something altogether different.

WHY CULTIVATE A LARGE PORTFOLIO OF BETS?

When established corporations consider new business ventures, they do so through enterprise lenses, often thinking, "We'll need to shell out $50 million just to get going." Those ventures are evaluated through market research and risk assessments in known markets, but even if they seem like winners in theory, they can still tank in practice. Which means that the C-level leaders who have been tapped to sit on their respective Growth Boards often resist the "large portfolio of bets" thesis. They envision shelling out billions to fund ideas that may fail spectacularly (or worse, never die at all, becoming zombies that suck up cash and resources yet never show anything for it).

So first, we introduce them to the Validation methodology we walked you through in the last chapter. And then we talk about the (surprisingly small) amount of capital the Validation process takes, and talk diversification.

When most execs hear the word *portfolio*, they immediately think "stocks." Which is understandable, since the idea of a diversified portfolio was first introduced to manage risk in investments in the stock market. But in the venture capital world, "portfolio theory" has a different connotation. Returns on venture capital are far too erratic to follow a traditional bell curve. Instead, they follow highly concentrated "power-law" distributions: In a typical VC fund, 65 percent of investments lose money, 25 percent provide a moderate return, and only 10 percent actually make the big bucks, according to Correlation Ventures, a VC fund.[1] In fact, the top 6 percent of VC investments appear to account for 60 percent of total profits, according to Horsley Bridge, a limited partner in many top VC funds.[2]

Let that sink in for a minute. Then consider how *incredibly* unlikely it is that you'd stumble on a venture that falls within that tiny 6 percent if you only invest in ten startups (let alone that one "Hail Mary" idea you were thinking of launching with tens of millions of dollars).

Because there is so little we know about new commercial spaces, we hedge risk by trying a lot of things. But we try them as cheaply as possible. Diversification in venture capital, therefore, should be geared toward learning—increasing the odds that those rare winners might be in the portfolio at all—rather than just optimizing toward financial outcomes of a single bet. Remember "ladders to the moon" from chapter 4? A portfolio of bets allows you to learn asynchronously and asymmetrically, increasing your chances of hitting it out of the ballpark. In enterprises, we see every project being pressed to deliver financial success; in VCs, we assume most investments— most new startups—will be duds, so we place *a lot* of bets.

This feels really different. We get that. Embracing volatility can be deeply uncomfortable for executives who have built their careers by being the best at optimizing and decreasing the risk of operations.

But here's why we're taking this approach: Applying traditional portfolio theory to enterprise growth efforts can be the kiss of death for large, established companies. Robert H. Hayes and William J. Abernathy saw this back in 1980 when they wrote an article titled "Managing Our Way to Economic Decline" for *Harvard Business Review*. They said:

> Originally developed to help balance the overall risk and return of stock and bond portfolios, these principles have been applied increasingly to the creation and management of corporate portfolios—that is, a cluster of companies and product lines assembled through various modes of diversification under a single corporate umbrella.

> When applied by a remote group of dispassionate
> experts primarily concerned with finance and
> control and lacking hands-on experience, the
> analytic formulas of portfolio theory push
> managers even further toward an extreme of
> caution in allocating resources.[3]

Our point? This kind of dispassionate calculation of ROI for new opportunities will never drive disruptive growth. It's the right tool for harvesting cash cows or evaluating sustaining innovations in core products. But to create new markets, leverage new enablers, and broaden their aperture on the future of the company, executives have to think beyond business-as-usual financial ratios.

Because success in a world that is unknowable requires three things:

1. A large volume of bets (that allow you to . . .)

2. Find the right solution

3. At the right time

So what, exactly, will the Growth Board do? And how does it help create and manage this diversified portfolio of bets? Let's start by defining the GB's three responsibilities.

THE GROWTH BOARD'S THREE RESPONSIBILITIES

Members of the Growth Board serve as investors, sounding boards, and diplomats. Their purpose is to enable the progress of in-process startups by outlining objectives, providing resources, and clearing roadblocks for the various on-the-ground teams.

Responsibility 1: Set growth goals

The first responsibility of a Growth Board is to define clear growth goals for the company. Those goals typically fall into several buckets:

- **REVENUE:** Are we seeking a certain revenue goal, and over what time period? (E.g., $1 billion in new revenue within five years? Three $50 million businesses within three years?) Spoiler alert: Almost all our partners set goals at the beginning of our pilots. And by the end of the pilot, when they really understand what it takes to do this work and what New to Big can do for them, they reset their goals. It's okay. While it's important to have a clear target from the beginning, it is just as important to understand that you'll likely have to change it once you get started.

- **MARKET:** Do we want to leverage the Growth OS to go after core, adjacent, or transformational opportunities? How can those opportunities support the organization's strategic objectives? Are we looking to enter a specific new market? Which market forces are having the greatest impact on our company?

- **ORGANIC/INORGANIC:** Do we want to focus on organic bets (ideas created inside the company), inorganic (VC investments in outside startups and/or mergers and acquisitions), or both? If both, what percentage of our resources and effort are we willing to allocate to each? (This strategy is strongly connected to the size and time frame of your growth goals.)

- **TIME HORIZON:** When considering technologies or enablers, some are near-term and some are much further

INVEST LIKE A VC **129**

out; how far into the future do we want teams to look? (How patient or impatient can you be?) And are there areas, business models, or customer segments that the company *won't* pursue?

Responsibility 2: Manage portfolio health

In order to effectively manage its portfolio, the Growth Board needs to be able to measure its health. But remember that traditional Big to Bigger metrics like IRR don't apply here! (Nor do stock market portfolio metrics like the Sharpe ratio or alpha.) Instead, we've defined four components that together create a snapshot of the portfolio's health: Focus, Size, Quality, and Velocity.

1. **FOCUS** speaks to the alignment with growth goals (core, adjacent, disruptive). As in, are all bets in the portfolio oriented toward the growth goals the board has previously defined for this work?
2. **SIZE** measures whether the portfolio has enough bets to hit its goals. Are the number of OAs and number of ideas within each OA large enough to overcome the odds of failure among the seeded startups?
3. **QUALITY** assesses the quality of the teams, the OAs, and strength of the proprietary gifts being leveraged, among others. This metric helps us determine if course-correction is needed from a staffing or investment thesis perspective.
4. **VELOCITY** measures the speed that the startups you have bet on are moving through the stages of the investment funnel, and the frequency that the funnel gets refilled with new ideas (i.e., new startups).

"We developed a growth thesis for each one of the business [units]," said Eric Gebhardt, former CTO for GE's Oil & Gas division. As Oil & Gas tracked startups in their portfolio, they consistently asked, "What phase is it in? Is it in seed? Is it in launch? Is it in grow? Where do we need to seed new things? Does it still fit the growth thesis? Are we balanced in our portfolio?"

Responsibility 3: Enable growth capability

The Growth Board must model the Growth OS mind-sets (as discussed in chapter 4) and give permission for teams to tell the commercial truth. They must understand and remove roadblocks inside the organization. And they must identify and encourage the right talent to drive New to Big growth. Ultimately, they enable growth capability both through how they talk about the work being done, and through the actions they take to support the people who are executing that work. Here's an example of what that looks like in practice:

When Bionic first started working with Tyco in 2013, CEO George Oliver was skeptical. We were brought in by the chief innovation officer, who was frustrated by the lack of a pipeline for new endeavors. He assumed Bionic would facilitate the funding process. Oliver needed his arm twisted, and sat grudgingly through the first Growth Board meeting. But by the second meeting, he was starting to see the light, and by the third he was a true believer.

At that third meeting, an OA cofounder was scheduled to present, and she was absolutely terrified. Her OA had initially appeared to have tremendous momentum, but once her team dug deeper, it proved to be a dud. Her task that day was to tell the Growth Board that the OA had been invalidated, and that the company should stop funding it. We coached her and encouraged her and reminded her that telling the commercial truth about the project was gospel, but she was still a mess. Which is understandable, since she had to step into a giant wood-paneled boardroom packed with C-level execs and explain that her team had bet on this project and lost.

She gave her presentation honestly and humbly that day. And on the spot, Oliver decided to promote her, because he understood how much courage it took to show that level of candor. That was the strongest signal he could give that he supported the Growth OS, through both success and failure. By doing that—especially around an opportunity that had so much early momentum behind it—he told all of Tyco that it was okay to try and fail. With his actions he told his entire company that they had permission to experiment, even if the process led them to some dead ends, because dead ends that were reached quickly and without huge investments saved them a ton of money and let them refocus their effort on the ideas that have potential.

Now that we've set the three responsibilities of the Growth Board, allow us to introduce two essential board members: the CEO and the External Venture Partner (EVP).

THE CEO *MUST* OWN THE GROWTH BOARD

Because New to Big growth requires leadership and teams to challenge age-old practices, it can only succeed if that change is led by senior leaders, and the CEO in particular. *This is nonnegotiable.*

Adopting New to Big mind-sets and investment criteria in any organization is challenging. It requires conviction that this is the *only* way to secure the company's future. It needs the permission to take risks that only the CEO and senior leadership can grant. If the CEO doesn't personally drive New to Big growth, guess what? No one else will, either. No news there.

We learned this lesson the hard way. In the past, we worked with partners where the CEO believed they could delegate growth. In each case, this attitude sent a clear message to the company: "This is something I want you all to do, but I am busy with more important things."

You can imagine how well those efforts turned out. Because the truth is, the leadership is at least half the reason big organizations can't grow at will. Every mind-set we unpacked in chapter 4 is the opposite of how top execs have been trained to think. They got to where they are by being right! By derisking! By following decades of best practices! By applying rigorous financial metrics to any new investment! They are expert operators! And now they have to learn to be creators, too?

If they want growth, yes.

Maybe this is you. (If so, we hope you'll finish the book instead of turning it into a doorstop right about now.) Or maybe this is your boss, or your boss's boss. (If that's the case, we hope you can extend them a bit of empathy—the rules are changing so quickly and they have to navigate such strange waters here.)

In either case, learning to be ambidextrous in your leadership—to be both an operator and a creator—is crucial for your continued success. Because it is no longer good enough to be a good leader; the twenty-first-century CEO must be a *growth* leader, and that starts with owning the Growth Board. Full stop.

BUILDING OUT THE TEAM

Now that we have the CEO on board, it's time to flesh out the rest of the Growth Board. The ideal size is between six and eight executives, with a mix of commercial and financial execs (technology, finance, legal, etc.) who have the moral, financial, and strategic authority to make Growth Board decisions. The goal is to assemble a board large enough to represent a range of perspectives, but small enough to be nimble and decisive.

SAMPLE GROWTH BOARD

GROWTH BOARD "Permissions & Funding"	CEO	CMO	CFO	COO	CTO	R&D	BU Pres	EVP

In our work with corporations, we also invite ourselves onto the Growth Board. (Hi.) Because to do this right, you need an outsider to help you vet ideas. Adam Grant shares a story in his book *Originals* that explains why.[4]

One of his former doctoral students, Justin Berg, did some research on people's ability to predict the success of new ideas. In one series of experiments, Berg, who is now on the faculty at Stanford's Graduate School of Business, asked circus artists (yes, circus artists—stay with us) to assess how likely their performances would succeed with audiences.

It turns out that the creators themselves were terrible at predicting the success of their own acts. They were too close to the ideas. So Berg gathered up some experienced circus managers and showed them videos of these new acts, and he asked the managers to predict which would be most loved by audiences. And in his research, he found that the managers weren't very good at idea selection, either. They had a prototype in their head of what they thought a good circus act would look like, and these acts just didn't fit that prototype.

But Berg wasn't done: He ran one more experiment.

He asked circus artists to assess acts that weren't their own— that is, he got fellow creators to weigh in as outsiders and judge the potential acts. And you know what? They were great at it. Their predictions were closest to the audience's actual feedback. Why? Because, Grant points out, creators tend to be too positive about their own ideas. And managers are too negative; they are trying to evaluate if the idea fits into their vision of what success looks like. But peer creators—outsiders—are more likely to look at an unusual idea and say, "This is totally different from anything I've seen, but it just might work." And they're also equally willing to say, "Nope, this is really bad. Go back to the drawing board and try again."

Bionic has assembled and sat on over a hundred Growth Board meetings over the years, and we've learned the hard way that each board absolutely *must* have an outsider's perspective. So we embed an External Venture Partner (EVP) on the Growth Board to bring an outside creator's perspective on all potential startup bets.

The EVP role is crucial for a successful Growth Board *specifically because* the EVP is an outsider to the company. Research shows that outsiders can be more creative because they are not constrained by traditional thinking and existing solutions.[5] They also give independent input and can de-politicize interactions because they have no existing bias toward the situation and essentially no stake in its outcome. To overcome cognitive—and institutional—biases, a knowledgeable, objective outsider is essential.

As you assemble your own Growth Board, look to your corporate board for an experienced entrepreneur and early-stage investor who could play the EVP role. Or you might look to your local startup ecosystem for an investor you could recruit to play this role. (Of course, you could also call us.) But the outsider role is the other nonnegotiable member of a successful Growth Board.

THE EVP BRINGS THE OUTSIDE IN

Allow us to be blunt: Executives are stubborn. Many of them have decades of experience across multiple industries, are used to making multimillion-dollar decisions every day, and believe they've pretty much seen it all. They are seasoned and wise, but also headstrong and intractable. Teaching them to transform how they think about new business endeavors can be arduous. Painful, even.

Luckily, they also love a good challenge. Rerouting old behaviors and beliefs is crucial to the Growth Board's success, so we look to the EVP to counsel the other board members, give them a healthy dose of entrepreneurial perspective, and often provide one-on-one coaching.

The EVP also works to steer members away from ingrained leadership behaviors that might quash the entrepreneurial process. They help execs learn to bring a beginner's mind to the table, asking questions instead of making statements and jettisoning calcified institutional biases. Every Growth Board needs a member who can examine the evidence with a view unclouded by internal politics and who can keep the group accountable for this new way of working. Without an outsider, it's hard to make the real shift from venture portfolio theory to practice.

The EVP must be someone who has been deeply embedded in the startup world, and therefore has a clear view of the business landscape outside the company's walls. Look for someone with experience as an early-stage investor and who has had at least one success *and* one failure as an entrepreneur. They bring context for new technologies, reconnaissance from the startup trenches, and coaching when execs stray away from New to Big mind-sets. And to the point about circus artists, they have been in both the startup "tent" as entrepreneurs and the early-stage investing "tent" long enough to be really good at evaluating new ideas.

INTRODUCING EXECUTIVE SPONSORS

Last, but certainly not least, you'll need Executive Sponsors. These key players don't usually sit on the Growth Board, but they play a vital role in bridging the Validation work of the cofounders and the investment work of the Growth Board. Their role is to push cofounder thinking, ensure the rigor of Validation, and remove roadblocks.

You might think of the Exec Sponsor as the partner at a VC firm who led the investment in a specific startup. While the full VC partnership (the Growth Board) voted to make the investment, the individual partner has the closest involvement with the team. They are the one the team calls when disaster strikes, or when they have surprising data that could lead to a pivot, or when they need help finding a subject-matter expert to advise them. And when it's time for the startup to raise another round of financing, they come back to the full VC partnership, but it's the individual partner who knows the most about the startup during the closed-door deliberations.

Early-stage investor Chris Sacca was well-known for only investing in startups where he knew he could affect the outcome in some way. While he was well aware that startups were inherently risky, "I knew that, for our companies, when stuff started going sideways, I could show up and be helpful. I could start to diagnose the problem. I could bring in better people to hire. I could help streamline the product road map. I could land their first couple of customers," he told us recently. As a result, he felt that "while success may be lucky, it's not an accident." That's a perfect way to think about the role of the Executive Sponsor.

In the context of an enterprise, the Executive Sponsor also becomes a hybrid startup board member and coach for the three OA cofounders, approving funding for individual Validation experiments, ensuring those experiments are sound, and confirming that team members are making evidence-based decisions as they progress.

Here's an example of the power of a great Exec Sponsor. At one of our partner companies, a team had been working on a new hair-care product for several years. They had identified a new use for an existing technology that would solve a real, painful customer need, and they wanted to launch this new product under one of their (beloved) existing brands. The company assigned a very senior R&D exec to sponsor the team, and being from R&D, the sponsor was less invested in any specific brand.

Using the Growth OS Validation methodology, the team quickly learned that customers did indeed want to solve this problem, but they wanted a solution that was both health-oriented (which their existing brand could offer) and beauty-oriented (which it could not). The team quickly realized they had no choice: They had to create a new brand to launch this new product successfully. But they were concerned that the Growth Board wouldn't like this answer. The Exec Sponsor allayed their fears, confirming that the commercial truth mattered more than any brand bias, and he supported their recommendation to the Growth Board to go ahead with this solution *only* if they did so under a new brand.

LAUNCHING A GROWTH BOARD

Now that you've got your roster of players, what are the rules of the game? Based on our experience across dozens of Growth Boards, we've developed a few principles to help you get up and running.

First Things First

1. **NO ATTENDANCE, NO VOTE:** Only Growth Board members in attendance may vote; no delegates/proxies allowed.
2. **FREQUENT MEETINGS:** Growth Boards should meet

at least once a quarter (as the number of OA teams increases, a subgroup may also meet more frequently).

3. **FACT-BASED:** Growth Boards must overcome their biases about what the "right" answer is and kill any inclination to support pet projects. Instead they must use the evidence uncovered by teams to make decisions.

4. **ACTION-ORIENTED:** Growth Boards must make go/no-go decisions at the meeting. Requests for follow-ups, additional opinions, etc., should be the exception, not the rule.

5. **REAL-TIME FEEDBACK:** OA teams should receive Growth Board decisions immediately following the Growth Board meeting; no keeping them in limbo.

Ground Rules

It's not easy to be the CEO of a multibillion-dollar company and hold back opinions in meetings. We get it. But the Growth OS requires everyone on the Growth Board to embrace a new style of leadership that's rooted in the practice of asking questions. The ground rules for board members employing question-based leadership are:

- Ask questions of the teams, rather than state opinions
- Ask questions appropriate to the stage of development
- Focus on the evidence the teams present
- Remain open to learning at all times
- Commit to trusting the teams and letting the evidence guide decisions

Addressing Mechanics and Cost

Once Growth Board members have made their peace with asking questions instead of assuming they already have the answers, they need to wrap their heads around *which questions* to ask. At the seed stage, those questions are not "What's the ROI?" "What are the margins?" or "What market share can we capture?" They're not questions that orbit RONA, ROIC, and IRR. Why not? Because those answers are unknowable this early and will remain so for a few years. Any attempt to answer them would produce intellectually dishonest results.

Instead we equip them with a list of questions that *are* knowable at each stage of a solution's development: At the earliest stages, those questions include "What are the most critical assumptions to test next?" "Tell me about the most passionate community or audience you've found for this idea," and "Who are the top competitors for this solution?"

As bets move through the Validation process, the questions shift more toward "What are the customer's top three priorities?" "What's the initial business model for this solution?" "What are the four or five inputs for that business model (LTV,* CAC,** etc.)?" and "What adjacencies make this a scalable business?"

While the Growth Board is mulling over those questions, it's important to circle back to mechanics. Board members know they'll be guiding the funding process, but often need reminding that their guidance won't be in the form of signing million-dollar checks. Not yet, anyway. At first, they'll cut their teeth making smaller investments in stages. Which can be counterintuitive to executives who are used to handing out massive pots of money, crossing their fingers,

---

* (Customer) Life Time Value

** Customer Acquisition Cost

and waiting a couple of years to see how it all pans out. It's easier for most executives to make a $10 million decision than a $100,000 decision.

Now they need to adjust to smaller risks in larger batches. They need to allot less money, but be prepared to see quick-turn, slightly messy results and make high-level judgment calls based on the evidence collected. They are empowered to cease funding if the OA teams come back with decidedly dismal results, but also required to hold any results to a new standard. When the team comes back in twelve or sixteen weeks to present their findings, those findings will not be slickly packaged or thoroughly derisked. But they will reveal evidence-based learning about the customer need and whether a proposed solution actually meets it. Growth Board members must be willing to trust the teams and trust the process.

Since the cost of being wrong is much lower in this management approach, many board members adjust quickly—sometimes *too* quickly—to the new paradigm. Making the switch from slow and costly to quick and cheap can be a little heady. It's easy to get excited about individual ideas and lose sight of the overarching Total Addressable Problem (TAP).

Here's what that might look like: A few years back, a Bionic EVP was working with a partner who got swept up in doing dozens of experiments on a fleet of diverse solutions. She had to rein in the process, saying, "It's fantastic that all these tests are yielding valuable learning, but what's the larger goal? What are they telling us about the bigger customer problem we're looking to solve?"

The team didn't *really* know. They were so thrilled by this quick-turn, high-yield system that they had lost sight of the higher goal. They felt like they were making progress, since they were getting a steady stream of tangible results, but they'd forgotten what they wanted to make progress *toward*.

The Growth Board stepped back and consolidated their learning about what constituted the biggest customer pain point. Remember that the teams were meant to be exploring a brand-new solution to a high-level problem in a way that would create an entirely new market. One that the company would own. Entirely. With that in mind, the EVP helped them reframe their OA, and a growth thesis emerged.

The company was able to say, "We're not going to market as a product manufacturer. We're going to market as the way to help our customers solve this massive problem. We're going to address this problem for a customer who is resource-constrained: one who has no room for an appliance, no time to solve the problem themselves, and no money to outsource the labor. We're going to create mechanisms that solve the problem in a way that is safe for their families and sustainable for the environment."

Working through mechanics and cost with the Growth Board is a journey. First there's hesitation, then understanding, then buy-in around the Growth OS methodology, then giddy excitement over snowballing team results, then reframing, and finally a crystallization of the larger growth thesis. It's a powerful, galvanizing experience for the Growth Board. They realize they're not just hammering away at new products to take to market; they're refining a vision for how they can address massive, ongoing consumer needs and, in doing so, build the future of the company.

Ready to observe an actual Growth Board meeting? Let's crack open that door and see what they're up to.

LIGHTS, CAMERA, ACTION!

We've covered all the pieces: the members, the mechanics, the methodology, and the long-term vision for the Growth Board. Now it's time to run through what these meetings look like. (Remember: This is *not* your typical investment committee meeting.)

Growth Board meetings are held quarterly, and typically take a half day. The primary purpose of the meeting is for the board to talk to the OA teams to understand what they are learning about the problems they are trying to solve, identify what the Growth Board can be doing to help them move faster, and make decisions for the portfolio going forward. The cadence for each team presentation is "Here's our hypothesis. We're going to go run these experiments to see if it's true. And we're asking you to tell us if we have permission to go after X or that we need Y to be able to move faster," rinse, and repeat. The board must then decide if they want to continue investing in the OA.

To kick it off, an OA's Executive Sponsor will typically spend a few minutes updating the Growth Board before the cofounders give their presentation. This stage-setting is a high-level executive summary: "Here's what we believe to be true. We've had these great insights, we believe X is a great opportunity, we're learning that Y doesn't have sufficient potential." This preps the board for what they're about to see. (As you likely know, execs like to start with the headline before they dig into details.)

One Growth Board meeting typically includes multiple OA team presentations, so it's the job of the board's EVP to keep things moving. Each team is given time to present their findings and for the board to ask questions. Teams may show videos of beachhead customers they've interviewed, demos of customers interacting with the prototypes, or mockups of their next stage of development. They may present data from other startups that have tested ideas in the same space, and results from their own experiments week over week. If teams believe a solution to be viable, they need to back that belief with solid findings and be prepared to defend their ask.

(In early Growth Board meetings, every OA team may come and present. But as the volume of bets in an OA increases, only teams that have a specific ask or need the Growth Board's sign-off to get additional funding and move further down the funnel should be presenting at any given meeting.)

Part of the work of the team, led by the Exec Sponsor, should be tracking the activity in the OA that's happening outside the company's walls. Where is funding going? Who are the incumbents and the rising players in the space? As part of their presentations at the Growth Board meeting, the Exec Sponsor and cofounders can request funding for an acquisition to accelerate their velocity within the OA.

Once the team leaders have wrapped up their presentations, the Growth Board and EVP head into closed-door discussion. The board reviews the decisions that need to be made about the various OAs and collects feedback for the teams. They'll decide whether to continue supporting the OA for another period of time (usually six to twelve months)—whether through funding, acquisitions, permissions, connections, or a combination thereof. And they'll look at their portfolio metrics and discuss whether they feel confident that their OAs have the volume, velocity, quality, and type of startup bets to achieve their growth goals.

After all OA teams have presented and the decisions have been made, the group will wrap with some self-reflection: How did they show up as a Growth Board? Did they ask the right questions? How could they improve next time?

Speaking of "next time," it's worth noting that although all Growth Board meetings follow the same basic format, the dynamics shift depending on how mature the Growth OS is within the organization. The very first Growth Board meeting is awkward and uncomfortable. For everyone. Both board members and OA teams are still on a pretty steep learning curve, so all parties are feeling self-conscious and off-balance. That's to be expected. (The EVP really drives this first session.)

The second Growth Board meeting—which is typically around

the six-month mark—runs a bit smoother. The teams have acclimated to their workflow and are starting to see some validation of their hypotheses. A few ideas may have already passed through Seed 1, or even Seed 2, and potential business models are starting to percolate. A few early front-runner solutions may have been tested using higher-fidelity prototypes.

By the third Growth Board meeting, there's often a solution making its way through Seed 3 that could be ready for the build stage. A few other ideas that are performing well in Seed 2 are being prepped to start Seed 3. By this point, the Growth Board now understands how to evaluate individual solutions, and while their portfolio may still be fairly small, they can begin to shift focus toward managing portfolio health.

Once the fourth Growth Board meeting rolls around, everyone is actually talking about and collaborating as a single investment body. With larger funding amounts at stake, the Growth Board discussion is focused on laying the groundwork for the new businesses ready to jump from the seed stages to the build stage, and the board is understanding the real-world economics of the market they're in (or about to create). By this point, the EVP is really stepping back from leading the Growth Board through the mechanics of the meeting and is instead acting as a trusted advisor to help them make the right investment decisions and manage the health of their growth portfolio.

REPLACING ONE-OFF WITH ALWAYS ON

Fostering a pro-entrepreneurship environment is one of the biggest and most important challenges Growth Boards face, often even more critical than facilitating funding. It involves providing organizational air-cover and freedom of operation for the OA teams, but also modeling creator mind-sets. Successful Growth Boards drive a high-speed and high-volume pipeline of bets by fostering an open-minded and risk-taking environment, anticipating and resolving roadblocks, providing the necessary resources, and focusing on the right opportunities.

But to make this an always-on capability, the Growth Board and the OA teams need to enlist backup from some key professionals: their human resources team. Because the only way for the Growth OS to become ingrained in the DNA of the company is through people. So let's talk about people.

8

IT ALL COMES DOWN TO PEOPLE

NEW TO BIG CANNOT HAPPEN WITHOUT PEOPLE. NONE of this works without the energy and enthusiasm of smart, dedicated, imaginative, collaborative, visionary, beautifully flawed human beings.

And yet you might be wondering, *Do I have the right talent to pull this off? And even if they're out there, how do I find them? How do I extract them from their day jobs and re-deploy them without disrupting entire systems? And then how do I convince them that this work will be rewarding, not career-killing?*

That last question stems from a deeply ironic circumstance that has evolved over the last decade or so: When employees within large companies are reassigned to "innovation" teams, it can mean their career is slow-tracking or, worse, completely over at that company. While they're engaged with "innovation," they've been forgotten by the Big to Bigger promotion-generating machine. Some people go so far as to say that innovation departments are where careers go to die. Let's just take a moment to acknowledge how deeply screwed-up that is: Our current systems literally punish the brave souls who take risks to build new things. So even if you've got dozens of natural-born entrepreneurs in your employee pool, they might not be eager to step up.

But wait! There's more bad news! In a Big to Bigger organization, the people who succeed most are those who thrive on predictability and mitigating risk. But New to Big is about going into the unknown, looking around new corners, and pushing boundaries. In Big to Bigger, people get promoted for being right; in New to Big, success requires acknowledging what we don't know and asking the right questions in order to learn. This dichotomy means that high-performers in a typical Big to Bigger company have cultivated exactly the wrong operating behaviors for New to Big work. The talent you need to power the Growth OS probably isn't the talent that's risen through the ranks already; it might need to be ferreted out. And, more broadly, to do New to Big successfully, you need to adapt your people-management infrastructure to find, motivate, retain, reward, and grow that talent.

FIRST, FIND THE ICONOCLASTS IN HR WHO WANT TO PARTNER WITH YOU

The crux of this organizational work splits into two parts. First we'll need to adapt the current Big to Bigger people-management systems to support the new entrepreneur/cofounder job function. Every one of the mechanisms in the current Big to Bigger talent-management system needs to be evaluated through the lens of entrepreneurship and venture capital: talent identification, performance reviews, reporting structures, incentives, compensation, which behaviors are prized, and what kind of leaders are promoted. All of it will need to be modified a little, or maybe a lot. If this sounds like we're standing up a whole new HR infrastructure, well, that's partly right. Most adaptations will be small; others will feel nearly impossible. The good news is that we won't need to do this work all at once (but we'll need to start running small HR experiments right away).

The second half of the org work involves cultivating the skills and mind-sets that lead to entrepreneurial success in employees and leaders who show the most promise. Since the Growth OS work being done by employees is fundamentally different from their old work—and *especially* since they may be doing this new work side-by-side with coworkers who are still utilizing established company protocols—they will need training, coaching, and mentorship.

It should be apparent by now that to accomplish all of these goals, we will need a creatively minded partner in HR who can dedicate a good portion of their time to the Growth OS. If you're worried that recruiting the ideal person will be a nightmare, rest easy; we've seen time and again that when we find the right HR partner, they are not only challenged, but also delighted by doing this work.

THE FOUR PILLARS

To guide the org work, you and your HR best friend need to start off with some inspiration and provocation. We've developed four pillars of talent principles that are essential to successfully implementing the Growth OS.

Pillar 1: Players and promoters

In the world of theater, there are two key groups of people necessary to successfully produce a play: "players," which includes actors, designers, directors, and stage managers who are fully dedicated to the production at hand; and "promoters," which includes agents, artist managers, producers, and others who are integral to the success of the show but are also working on other projects simultaneously.

All people touched by the Growth OS have needs within the program and must be cared for, whether they are "all in," like players, or merely "involved," like promoters. Promoters need to be attended to, not ignored or made to feel left out. Part of our mandate is to gain their support, remove roadblocks, respect their needs, and, above all, avoid damaging their careers.

Pillar 2: It must be safe to try

Throughout the process, participants will be asked to do things that are unsupported by the status quo. They may be pulled from their departments, assigned new managers, and told to abandon projects that are in progress. Doing this takes *guts*. And if it doesn't work out, they need solid assurances that they will be taken care of. They know that abandoning their posts puts them at risk of being sidelined, and they are taking a mammoth risk by joining these teams. It's vital that they know they will not be punished, stalled, demoted, or replaced if they step up to contribute.

"We always thanked the teams for the learnings; the teams that got their funding cut were treated no differently than the teams that continued on," GE's Eric Gebhardt insisted. "They saw that it was a safe environment to do that, that it wasn't failure but validated learning. Building that trust was very important."

Likewise, those folks have managers—within matrixed organizations, who may be multiple managers—who are down a person, and may even be accountable for their employee's performance in that new role. (A role they have no visibility into, and no understanding of, by the way.) That's a risk they should not be asked to take. So do whatever you need to do to make those former managers safe. Nobody's career should be threatened by participation in the Growth OS program.

Pillar 3: Do the easy thing that's good enough

For the right HR person, this principle is the most freeing. Consider that HR people are in a challenging situation: The programs and policies they roll out affect tens or hundreds of thousands of people, all at once. If they get one thing wrong, it can feel like the world is coming down around their heads. So HR people have been trained from their first job out of college to create "comprehensive," "perfect," and "buttoned-up" solutions that work for the largest number of people.

Here we're inventing things that have never been tried before, but affect only twenty or thirty people at the beginning. It's not necessary to roll out a perfect solution that's scalable to tens of thousands of employees. In fact, that approach would be counterproductive! Instead, your HR partner should run small-scale experiments, just like the OA cofounders, because they're doing the same thing: trying to learn as quickly and cheaply as possible. Instead of massive, comprehensive, and bulletproof, find the easiest thing that gets enough of the job done so that HR can learn whether their imagined solution will work as intended.

Creating easy, short-term fixes to accommodate the new entrepreneur function may not give you scalable solutions for the long term. It will, however, create solutions that work for the immediate future, teach you a lot, and buy your team time to figure out what a permanent solution might look like.

Pillar 4: Value performance of the team over the individual

Entrepreneurship is a collective endeavor. This means that individual effectiveness is only valuable if it contributes to team effectiveness. This philosophy is the polar opposite of the one held by most big organizations, so it's important to note and absorb. It means that success is based on the group's progress toward the collective goal, rather than on an individual's contribution. In an early-stage startup, there are rarely performance evaluations—your company either continues to exist or it doesn't. You're either on the team or off. This reality creates laser focus on collective outcomes ("We only sold ten pairs of shoes today") rather than individual activity ("I made the marketing page on schedule").

Because the work, and how we hold participants accountable, is so different from the norm, it means that only leaders working within the Growth OS program are qualified to evaluate performance. Promoters may have opinions, but players are the ones who know what "good" means in this context.

Study these pillars and keep them top-of-mind as you shift your attention toward Growth OS team-building. Obviously your HR partner will need to be on board, but so will everyone else. Growth Board members and OA cofounders will need to adopt these philosophies for as long as they are engaged in this work.

Now let's discuss how to track down the right people to staff those teams.

CREATE OPPORTUNITY FOR ENTREPRENEURS IN HIDING

At the beginning of this work there is often a period of hand-wringing. Leaders say, "We don't have the right people to take on this work! No one in our company is doing anything like this."

Rest assured, you've got everyone you need on the payroll already. Deep within your organization there are employees with entrepreneurial sensibilities who are attracted to ambiguity, love to experiment, and are constantly imagining a better way to solve a problem. They are constant learners and are not afraid to challenge deeply held assumptions, which is why they are more often seen as "misfits" rather than candidates for high-potential programs. So your first step is to coax them out of hiding by demonstrating the career-changing potential of doing this work.

That coaxing is essential: If anyone is strong-armed into this work, it will lead to misery. You can't just tell someone, "Guess what? This is your job now." If they're not suited to entrepreneurial, growth-focused work, or if they're good at it but not passionate about it, they'll wither. (And resent the company for screwing up their career.) Ask, don't demand; solicit volunteers, don't draft unwilling participants.

Step 1: Screen for key traits

There's a seemingly never-ending stream of books and articles eager to tell you which attributes and talents are *always* present in successful entrepreneurs. But the attributes and capabilities we've assembled have been carefully calibrated to identify people equipped to do Growth OS work within an established company.

It may be tempting to bypass screening for these key traits if you've got a venerable, time-tested entrepreneur already on staff. This was the case with an early Bionic partner; a senior leader had won awards for his entrepreneurial endeavors, made a small fortune off the businesses he'd built before joining the organization, and been on staff for several decades. Naturally, the company assumed he was a perfect choice and placed him on the OA team without considering the cofounder attributes screener. It turns out that he was truculent and resistant, and his previous experience clouded his ability to accept new approaches. His team suffered, and so did the work. This earned him a quick exit from the Growth OS work, and the company realized that the key cofounder traits were nonnegotiable.

Here are the traits we seek in Growth OS participants, and that you can use within your own company to screen for natural entrepreneurial aptitude:

GROWTH BOARD MEMBER TRAITS

Growth Mind-Set: Believes deeply in the importance of entrepreneurship and is passionate about bringing concepts and best practices into the organization. Driven to create outcomes grounded in customer needs.

Resilience: Thinks in terms of possibilities and is comfortable working through ambiguity to achieve highest growth. Willing to take appropriate risks and make decisions in uncertainty. Comfortable with nonconsensus.

Question-Based Leader: Uses questions to drive toward clarity and commercial truth. Recognizes and rewards productive failure. Uses evidence to validate or invalidate critical assumptions.

Accountability: Reports directly to the CEO. Has the sphere of influence and authority required to remove barriers (organizational, cultural, systems, etc.).

Disruptor: Challenges status quo and deeply held cultural and organizational norms, cutting through bureaucracy to accelerate outcomes.

Grants Permissions: Creates an environment where all feel comfortable expressing conflicting opinions. Creates conditions where bold ideas, staring down hard truths, and taking smart risks can exist.

EXECUTIVE SPONSOR TRAITS

Catalyst: Models the growth mind-set and enables others to do so as well.

Passionate: Has an intense belief in the opportunity and a strong desire to provide an impactful solution.

Respected: Has enough tenure and authority to remove barriers and provide access to their teams.

Supportive: Provides teams with guidance (approximately one hour per week) and backing for their asks of the Growth Board.

Gardener: Takes an eyes-on, hands-off approach with teams, guiding them to the right resources without telling them the answer or managing the process.

COFOUNDER TRAITS

Adaptable: Invents novel approaches. Figures out what to do when ready-made processes or techniques are inadequate.

Curious: Finds patterns between disparate, seemingly unrelated sources anticipating innovative ways to build and position new business ideas.

Humble: Demonstrates continuous personal development with the team and desire to learn from others. Sees collaboration as a mechanism for self-improvement.

Passion for Experimentation: Adeptly layers together experimentation with other research, testing, and metrics to reveal strengths and flaws in the current strategy and devise a clear path forward.

ADDING COFOUNDER TEAMS & EXEC SPONSORS

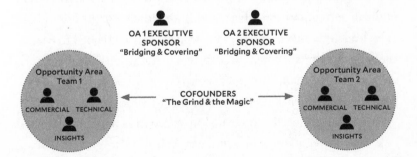

(There's one more team you'll need to staff—the Operations Team. We'll dig into them in the next chapter.)

As you collect names and interview interested candidates, make sure they have these characteristics or show the potential to adopt them. Doing this will ensure success for both the individuals and the projects they drive.

Step 2: Foster self-selection

As we mentioned earlier, "volun-telling" people into this work is a terrible move. It'll serve you far better to foster an environment that encourages folks with the desired traits to step up and volunteer.

The first move is for the CEO to become a Growth OS superfan.

If the messages from the top are positive and exciting, people are more likely to raise their hands. If the CEO is leading the Growth Board and vocally supporting this work, encouraging other senior leaders to follow suit, then talented employees will feel safe coming forward. Creating awareness and highlighting leadership's enthusiasm will lay the groundwork.

David Taylor, CEO of Procter & Gamble, has modeled this well. He has invested in an internal Growth OS program named GrowthWorks, sits on the Enterprise Growth Board, and models the behavior as a learning leader. Kathy Fish, chief research, development, and innovation officer, and Marc Pritchard, chief brand officer, lead GrowthWorks with a centralized team designed to enable the business units. People with entrepreneurial spirits across P&G are raising their hands to get involved in this type of work, and in the process are identifying new opportunities for growth.

The second move in fostering self-selection is to offer easy, low-risk ways for employees to volunteer. You want to give people an opportunity to experience and understand what these new jobs are like, and you want to keep a list. You might not have a spot for them today, but you might have one soon.

CONSIDER CREATING A GROWTH OS–SPECIFIC JOB FAIR.
Staff various stations with folks who can explain exactly what various roles will entail, and what participants will do at various stages of the process. Invite them to express interest, then put them on your watch list.

ANOTHER OPTION IS TO HOST A STARTUP WEEKEND.
Invite all interested employees to a two-day intensive retreat where they're given a prompt, asked to generate some ideas, and tasked with running a few tests. At the end of the weekend, each team pitches their solution. The goal is not to harvest actual business ideas; it's to find out who is both interested in and talented at entrepreneurial work. You don't need to give them all roles right away. Instead, you can create a pipeline of interested folks to draw from as you expand the work. (And, obviously, this doesn't have to occur on a Saturday and Sunday. Any two consecutive days will work.)

Step 3: Create safety for exploration

Earlier in the chapter, we mentioned that engaging in innovation work within a large company can be career suicide. Switching gears to focus on building new products or offerings has often been a potential career-limiting move, and one that many people actively fear. Once someone was uprooted from the core to work with an innovation team, they frequently weren't welcomed back *into* the core after the innovation team wrapped up its work. No one was advocating for them at talent calibration meetings because they weren't part of core teams. Their positions had often been backfilled. (And what if the innovation "failed"? Their "personal brand" within the core might have taken a hit.)

A few years back, we saw this happen to a Growth OS cofounder. She'd been selected from her position in the consumer insights department to focus on a new endeavor, but was still reporting to her old department manager. He had no idea what her new work entailed or how to evaluate her success, so he just stuck to the same performance expectations he'd been using for everyone else in his unit. She continually tried to explain the work she was completing and the skills she was learning, but her manager was totally unprepared to process it. She felt out to sea, and he felt ill-equipped to guide her. And once she had finished her Growth OS work, neither had any idea how to reintroduce her into the department or get her back up to speed. Think back to Pillar 2: Safe to Try. Because the organization wasn't fully prepared, it was not safe for either one of them to have her try the Growth OS assignment.

Now, we have said already that cofounders and all Growth OS staff need to report to their respective Executive Sponsors instead of their old supervisors. For the duration of this work, they need to be evaluated only by other people involved in the work. But we also make sure to build mechanisms that keep employees protected while they've stepped away from their current roles and departments.

To avoid turning the Growth OS into a regrettable career-limiting-move machine, companies must prepare from day one for people to return to the core. Not everyone will want to go back—many may find this entrepreneurship track a better fit for their skills and goals—but the off-ramp must exist for those who want it after a Growth OS tour of duty. That can mean creating a new sponsorship approach that assigns a senior leader and an HR partner who are close to the work to advocate for them. It can also mean crafting clear communications around how their new skills and mindsets will support the core once they've returned. The reentering employee will want the tools to evangelize the program and train others in the growth skills and mind-sets they have learned.

TALENT TRANSPLANT PROTOCOLS

While the Growth Board members and Exec Sponsors will add Growth OS work to their existing plates, it's critical that cofounders are fully dedicated to their OA work. For many, it will be on a temporary basis—eighteen months, two years, maybe a bit longer—but during that time, they must be 100 percent dedicated.

If an entrepreneur were only 30 percent dedicated to their startup, they would never be funded by a VC. Investors may take meetings with or offer advice to part-time entrepreneurs, but they would never write a check to back a founder who hadn't gone all-in themselves. This work cannot be a side project that only gets a fraction of anyone's time and attention. Here's why: Entrepreneurs need to obsess about the customer problems they are solving in order to uncover the insights that create massive commercial opportunity. And more to the point, in an enterprise, trying to do both jobs (Growth OS and core) creates conflicting incentives, and which one will get the front seat? The one you've been working on forever and that will determine your next promotion.

C-level and senior leadership have to champion 100 percent dedication and should be willing to go to bat to defend its importance. When that happens, people at all levels know it's safe to give their heart and soul to innovation work.

So you've screened a prospect, found her suited to the work, and granted her an OA cofounder role. How do you extract her from her current role, department, and workload?

There's no single right answer to that question, unfortunately, but we can definitely circle back to Pillar 3: Do the Easy Thing That's Good Enough. When you're just revving up that New to Big engine, you don't have to have a scalable HR protocol in place to take people out of existing roles and reassign them to OA teams without disruption. You just need to rig up a temporary system that will work for your first batch of innovators, which is usually a dozen people or fewer.

Maybe that means setting up all the OAs as a separate organization within the whole. Maybe that means moving all the cofounders to the same existing business unit temporarily. Your own corporate structure, payroll protocols, and HR systems will dictate what's possible and what's outlandish. Feel free to assemble a solution that will enable the work to begin, then dig into the details of how to make it scalable as the project progresses.

So far, so good. But what about the folks who *aren't* intimately involved in this venture-building work, but whose support is crucial to its ongoing success? What about those promoters—the former line managers of the newly minted cofounders, supporting functions like legal, finance, compliance, HR (basically anyone who can say no, but has nothing at stake for this work to succeed)—how do we support and engage them?

PROMOTER MANAGEMENT 101

Promoters who understand the value of Growth OS work and feel respected by the people doing it are happy promoters. And happy promoters don't make trouble for the people doing the Growth OS work.

Unhappy promoters, on the other hand, can be serious detractors.

We once worked with a partner where we kicked off the work as we always do: attracting cofounders, scoping out opportunity areas, and setting up OA teams to be 100 percent dedicated, with Exec

Sponsors serving as the new day-to-day manager for the cofounders. But in this company, the cofounders' former line managers were technically still responsible for them in the HR system; those former line managers were still on the hook for the cofounders' year-end reviews and for compensation and promotion recommendations. So they kept their weekly one-on-one meetings with the cofounders, and asked them for regular readouts, creating several hours of additional work for the cofounders each week. The cofounders didn't complain, but the extra work took a toll on them *and* made them concerned about their upcoming evaluation and compensation discussions, since their Growth OS work didn't neatly map to their divisions' development tracks.

After a month or two, one of the cofounders casually mentioned this concern to the Exec Sponsor, who was stunned; they didn't know this was going on, and they were understandably concerned about cofounder morale and focus. At the same time, they recognized how important it was to keep the former managers in the loop and to overcommunicate the experiences and skills the cofounders were developing in this work. So they looped in their Growth OS HR partner, and together, they sat down with the former managers to create a plan to give them monthly updates on the work, as well as greater transparency into the coaching and development plans for the cofounders. Then they scheduled time for everyone— including the cofounders—to talk about compensation and evaluation plans for the OA team so they felt safe to experiment, fail, and iterate.

And it worked like a charm. Exuberant support from a top leader combined with open, welcoming communication proved to be a highly effective promoter-management strategy. It is one that we've since adopted for other partners, and one that will likely work as you install the Growth OS in your own organization.

People fear what they don't understand, but when they feel

informed, they're less likely to lash out. It's crucial to be transparent and open about Growth OS work from the very start, especially because it is fundamentally different from typical corporate transformation efforts.

Longtime employees may have seen internal experiments before. Let's all embrace agile transformation! Or build our software differently! Or utilize lean techniques! Whatever it is, let's all do it together!

This is different. This is a small group of people who are wholly committed to a subset of work. And to catalyze that deep change, we draw a circle around those committed people. We might start with 30. By year two, it could grow to 150, which is still very small for a large organization. It's a tiny subset that appears, from the outside, to be getting special treatment and following special rules. People outside that circle are curious. They feel threatened. They want to know how, when, and if this little circle of people doing compartmentalized work is going to force them to change their own working habits. Is this a new wave coming, and if so, how do they prepare to ride it out?

The best way to inoculate against that fear is through open sharing of information, as the last example shows. And although top-level support and vocal buy-in are essential, so is recruiting an HR business partner. Having someone skilled in both communications and people management to help quell fears, manage rumor mills, and answer questions can be a lifesaver.

Speaking of HR, let's revisit Pillar 3 one more time, shall we? Do the Easy Thing That's Good Enough is an important mindset for internal HR staff to adopt as the Growth OS rolls out. If some subset of HR is open to being on a journey along with the OA teams and Exec Sponsors, if they embrace the idea that this is a grand experiment that they're taking part in, they'll see how they can contribute to this new operating system rather than feel dragged along with it. These folks will have the opportunity to design a new kind of talent management solution, one linked to a growth mind-set, and one that can be scaled. But also one that should be tinkered with, piloted, and tested on a small scale before a companywide rollout is implemented.

Once they see that we're not changing everybody—we're changing one teeny-tiny sliver of the company for a temporary period of time in order to validate something that could be more permanent—many HR team members are incredibly relieved. In fact, some find it to be a breath of fresh air and end up adopting experimentation quicker than other functions! HR folks are among the most important promoters, and getting their support is essential to making this organizational change possible.

REVISING REWARDS SYSTEMS

As the program matures, an important task is determining how New to Big work should be compensated and rewarded. We wish we had a one-size-fits-all formula you could plug into your current systems to translate Big to Bigger compensation into New to Big, but we just don't. Compensation and rewards are often both industry-specific and fantastically convoluted.

That said, here are some things to keep in mind as you customize your rewards systems to suit Growth OS work:

HOLD STEADY AT THE START: Participants' compensation should ideally be held unchanged for at least the first six months of the program. This gives everyone a chance to see if they are a good fit for the work. This also has the benefit of being easy to implement and good enough (see Pillar 3).

MAKE EXPECTATIONS CLEAR AT THE OUTSET: Since Growth OS participants will be evaluated based on new and different criteria, make sure they all know that from day one. For instance, Growth Board members will be held accountable for practicing question-based leadership and asked to improve if they choose to monologue endlessly instead. But they all need to know that ahead of time so they can adjust their behaviors accordingly.

GET INPUT FROM THE EXECUTIVE SPONSOR: To compensate everyone fairly, performance expectations need to be codesigned by someone who has a deep understanding of the work being done. Your HR partner should be sure to involve the Executive Sponsor.

DEFINE BOTH "GOOD" AND "BAD" CRITERIA: Since project failure is *not* to be feared throughout this process, it's essential to let people know which behaviors are considered detrimental. For instance, overbuilding a prototype might be a ding-worthy offense, while getting clear evidence from an underbudget experiment could be bonus-worthy behavior.

REWARD TEAMS, NOT INDIVIDUALS: Once again, this is work that must be done collectively. That means it needs to be rewarded collectively. Doing this motivates everyone to collaborate more effectively and enthusiastically.

COMMUNICATE SUCCESSES: Articulate when and why people within the Growth OS are being promoted. Deliberately tout these successes so that everyone within the company will know the work is being valued.

And, especially at the outset, be flexible and willing to make changes. A compensation system that made sense on paper may wreak havoc in practice. Find nonfatal ways to test your ideas, and welcome their failure. It's okay; we're all experimenting together, remember?

Being transparent is especially vital when it comes to recognition and rewards given to Growth OS participants because it impacts recruitment. If the company at large doesn't see this way of working as connected to career progression, it will be challenging to attract new volunteers when you're ready to expand. But if your employees can see clearly that working and operating in an entrepreneurial way can lead to personal growth, promotions, and raises, they will be thrilled to get on board.

MEASURING SUCCESS

Measuring success of the OA teams may seem pretty straightforward: If the solutions they test and eventually bring to market scale and become profitable, success!

But organizational success is more ephemeral. You want to be able to attract, retain, develop, and land the right people for the Growth OS. In order to do that, you need all the mechanisms of effective management—clear jobs, aligned pay, recognition, advancement potential, career growth, and a good understanding of what it takes to be successful. If your people are growing and succeeding in finding and building new businesses, then your organization is probably pretty good. If you end up with a thriving ecosystem of repeat entrepreneurs, then you've won.

Yes, you want your portfolio of solutions to be thriving, but the growth of the people managing that portfolio should be acknowledged, too. That growth, and the skills and wisdom that accompany it, often become gifts to the core.

When we worked with Nike, the company had identified and validated a real and ongoing need among schools to design and produce small batches of sports team uniforms and fan gear. So we began to explore a direct-to-consumer model, a way for schools to create and order just what they needed, with accessible pricing and quick turnaround times.

The team went pretty far down that road, mocking up what this new model might look like. But instead of launching it as a standalone business—which Nike could've done very easily—the company realized that there was little risk and lots of benefit to bringing that work into the core. So that's what they did—gifting this success to the entire organization. And it has literally changed the conversation for how the core team is functioning. The entrepreneur who had been leading it went on to explore another idea, bringing all her learning to the new OA.

When you're crafting your own organizational protocols, remember that there are multiple ways to measure success. If the core is changing and evolving because of Growth OS work, that can be absolutely priceless to the company overall. We've worked with many companies who hired us for growth outcomes, but reaped invaluable benefits back to the core in terms of innovative thinking and appreciation for the value of change. When they see the value in both, we know they've taken this work to heart.

Ultimately, this organizational work is the backbone of New to Big success. It empowers cofounders to be all in, supports Executive Sponsors to catalyze learning, and builds accountability for Growth Board members to become ambidextrous leaders.

So build that backbone first, then read on to chapter 9 to learn how to build a permanent New to Big capability throughout your company.

9

INSTALL A PERMANENT GROWTH CAPABILITY

So you've decided to do this. You believe in the Growth OS model, understand why you need both entrepreneurs and VCs inside your company, and trust that your executives can become ambidextrous leaders. Excellent! Before you begin installing the Growth OS inside your organization, you need to define what success looks like—that is, what do you hope to accomplish by creating an entrepreneurial engine within your organization?

In most cases, the large-scale goals that companies set around innovation fall into one of two categories:

NEW GROWTH: Success here is defined by the number of new businesses that your company launches into market. You want to ramp up growth by introducing innovative, consumer-centric offerings. You want lots of bets, a healthy ROI, and PR-worthy proof that your organization isn't stuck in stasis.

GROWTH CAPABILITY: Success here is defined as creating systems, tools, and structures that enable portfolio-building to happen on an ongoing basis. You want to empower your organization to create with consumer pain points in mind. You want your executives to become ambidextrous leaders: both operators and creators. And you want your organization to be nimble enough to support both New to Big and Big to Bigger. Because while you're definitely keen to increase the number of profitable, large businesses that your company launches, your primary goal is building sustainable mechanisms and culture to make that increase repeatable.

Put more bluntly, do you want fish, or do want to learn how to fish?

Spoiler alert: We hope you want to do both. Yes, you need growth, and that should always be the primary driver, but the real value is building the machine that allows you to reliably generate that growth, over and over and over. Sure, you could form a team, spawn a couple dozen groundbreaking ideas, enter a new market, and beta-launch a new offering in the next year. But wouldn't you rather build a machine that can launch an entire portfolio of offerings *every year*?

It's a pretty appealing proposition, but that doesn't mean everyone in your entire organization will get on board to adopt growth capability from day one. "Let's pilot this new way of working with a small group for a set amount of time and see what happens!" is much easier to sell than "Let's change the way our entire multibillion-dollar company works forever and ever!" In no small part because your current setup has been designed and refined to handle its current workload.

The human systems that you have installed within your organization are designed for Big to Bigger work. Your e-commerce platform, sales strategy, and marketing machine are all calibrated for Big to Bigger. Your manufacturing, packing, and logistics systems are engineered for Big to Bigger. And, perhaps most important, the ways your executives think and make decisions foster predictable profitability in a Big to Bigger world. In all likelihood, everything about your company has been constructed to support low-risk, low-variation growth, not disruptive, market-creating, New to Big growth.

As Harvard Business School professors Clayton Christensen and Stephen Kaufman point out in their Resources, Processes, and Priorities (RPP) framework, "the very capabilities that propel an organization to succeed in sustaining circumstances will systematically bungle the best ideas for disruptive growth. An organization's *capabilities* become its *disabilities* when disruption is afoot."[1]

Jud Linville, the former CEO of Citi's credit cards business unit, acknowledged this dichotomy in his advice to leaders considering this way of working: "The first thing is to understand that any organization is going to be resistant at first because you've got built-in processes and platforms and people who are hardwired to do things. So understand the resistance, honor the resistance, and then specifically address the resistance." He continued, "The second piece is, starting early on in the process, determine the different control breakers that prevent your organization from moving fast. Acknowledge and affirm that they're there to protect your institution at scale. And then communicate very clearly to the organization how the New to Big work will not threaten those controls if you construct the right test kitchen."

When we think about growth capability, we think about taking all these mechanisms inherent to the organization that are built for Big to Bigger maintenance and objectives, and reconfiguring them in a limited way to make this new, different body of work possible.

You're creating a "test kitchen," as Linville puts it, that's dedicated entirely to New to Big development, all the while preparing the systems and culture inside the rest of the organization to repeatedly take any successes and turn them into massive wins. The goal here isn't the test kitchen itself, but the capability to create new growth on a permanent, ongoing basis.

Whatever your goals may turn out to be, you must make them explicit at the outset of this work. If you've got Growth Board members saying, "I want growth and revenue," and Exec Sponsors saying, "I want capability and learning," while the promoters are saying, "I want things to go back to the way they were," you will stall. Creating clarity and agreeing on goals is the single most important thing you can do to set up this work for success.

So with clear goals in hand, you're ready to install and launch the Growth OS, right? Well, not quite yet. There's one more key team that needs to be assembled before the discovery and experimentation fun begins.

HOW DO YOU KNOW IF YOU'RE READY TO TRY THIS?

You're the drummer in a jazz combo, and you've recently decided that your current band should switch to a classic rock playlist. You may feel 100 percent ready to kick-start that change, having studied and practiced and scoped out venues and done research proving that playing classic rock will pay better. But if you haven't discussed the idea with your bandmates, if they have never dabbled in this new-to-them genre, if they love jazz and fear change, you've got a bloody, uphill battle ahead of you. It doesn't mean you won't convince them, but you might have to spend a long time and a lot of effort getting them on board.

Similarly, if you're the sole person (or department) in your company who is thrilled at the prospect of bringing in entrepreneurship and VC mechanics to manage new endeavors, you will struggle. It doesn't mean you won't succeed, but you might have to spend a long time and a lot of effort laying essential groundwork. And by the time you have enough support, you may be too exhausted to care, much less forge ahead.

So to get a sense of both your and your company's readiness, ask yourself how many of these statements are true:

- You've read about Lean Startup methodology (probably before you picked up this book).
- You've tried some experiment-based learning yourself, ideally in your current position or at your current company.
- At least a few of your leaders are vocally excited about incorporating some new innovation strategies and working tactics.
- You have pockets of startup-like activity within your company, but they lack an organizing framework.
- You've been looking outside the walls of your organization for inspiration and guidance (books, conferences, speakers).
- You can see the threats to your business from competitors or other outside forces, and your leadership is starting to sense the urgency to act.
- **Bonus:** Your organization recently hired a new leader

who hails from the startup/technology world (or at least an outsider whose career wasn't built by rising through ranks at your firm).

If you answered no to more than half those statements, you'll likely have an uphill battle ahead of you. But don't despair! Instead of abandoning this work altogether, focus on shoring up key support.

- Seed some of these ideas at the leadership level by inviting an outsider—veteran VC, serial entrepreneur, academic, or thought leader in this space—to your next offsite or leadership team meeting.
- Attend conferences to connect with and learn about companies who are leading the way. (And to introduce yourself! This work is far easier when you have peers to support you.)
- Visit startups in your industry and see how fast they go from concept to product to market, or from feature to beta test. Better yet, bring some of your leadership team with you to help drive home the point that speed beats size when it comes to discovering and validating new ideas.
- Check out the recommended reading and watching list in the Resources section at the back of this book.

THE OPS TEAM: YOUR DESIGNATED ROADBLOCK BUSTERS

Because Growth OS work is so different from typical corporate work, getting it started and pushing it through can be positively onerous. Frequently, companies lack the infrastructure necessary to support entrepreneurial-style work, and long-standing processes like budget sign-offs and matrix approvals slow everything to a glacial rate. Even if those issues can be bypassed, entire departments of people often stand in the way of this work.

Since New to Big needs to iterate quickly—and since the OA teams will be dedicated to discovering and experimenting with new business opportunities, with no free time to appease promoters or devise infrastructure—you need to create an Operations Team (or Ops Team, the drivers of the Growth OS). This is a group of creative problem-solvers with an aptitude for and interest in innovation. While it will be run by one or two dedicated leaders, you'll also recruit champions from key functions like legal, marketing, IT/security, finance, and, yes, compliance, folks whose support will grease the wheels. They're tasked with anticipating who or what will get in the way of this work, and ensuring it doesn't.

The Ops Team should also have a C-level Exec Sponsor who is dedicated to eliminating any roadblocks to growth work. This person is a bona fide communications ninja, someone who's been in the company for years, a gregarious type who knows everyone and knows how to get things done. This person is ultimately on the hook for delivering net new growth in the company. They will become the expert on all things New to Big.

The issues the Ops Team will tackle can be everything from bringing senior leaders along to ensure proper staffing of the OAs to proposing solutions to experimentation setbacks. For example, many OA teams choose to create mocked-up websites while testing their solutions. Since the sites are meant to collect data on user behaviors and preferences, some thorny legal issues can crop up. Any site that collects email addresses is required by law to disclose collection in a privacy policy. In California, additional tracking language must be included in the privacy policy to indicate if IP addresses are involved (SurveyMonkey, a tool we frequently deploy, collects IPs) or analytics information from individuals. Since the Ops Team typically includes a liaison from legal, that person can quickly draft boilerplate privacy policy language that works for the experiment and addresses the company's needs.

This is important: The Ops Team lead and Exec Sponsor should be in place before OA experimentation begins. Don't try to throw an Ops Team together after you've hit the first hiccup; the folks working through Discovery and Validation will need active support from day one. Be proactive, and build this barrier-busting team ahead of time.

Is this team really necessary? Can't the OA teams or their Exec Sponsors handle the issues and obstacles that crop up? Short answer: No, they cannot. Do not saddle the cofounders with running interference for themselves. If they have to negotiate permission from the support functions, that is all they will ever do. The actual experimentation and learning will get back-burnered and everything will grind to a halt. The Ops Team exists so that the OA teams can do their work quickly and cheaply, without organizational friction.

ADDING THE OPS TEAM

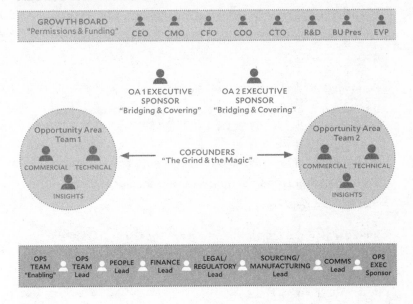

So before you even start brainstorming OAs and recruiting cofounders, pull together a team of roadblock busters. Their work paves the way to go fast.

OPS TEAM MEMBER TRAITS

Innovative: Isn't afraid to challenge the status quo, question assumptions, and generate new ideas by looking at issues from multiple angles.

Connector: Takes time to reflect on experiences, learnings, and insights. Spends focused energy processing this information, gaining deeper insights into consumer problems, solution possibilities, and new business models.

Catalyst: Isn't afraid to challenge the status quo in order to help teams identify and validate disruptive new growth opportunities.

Beacon: Is not only able to work in this iterative and unstructured environment, but also ready to provide support to teams throughout the process.

Mover of Mountains: Ready to identify and remove barriers, even when there is no clear process, and enable teams to reach their objectives.

Evangelist: Embodies the mind-sets of the Growth OS and socializes across the organization with whatever means necessary.

Now you're ready. You've done the prep, you've got key people in place on the Growth Board and Ops Team, and your OA cofounders are raring to go. Here's what the first phase of this new work will look like.

Phase 1: Configure a pilot

The most important piece of advice we can give you as you begin rollout? Start small. It's possible that you'll get so much internal pushback that starting small will be your only option, but on the off chance that your entire organization is instantly gung ho, be smart and dial it back. Don't put a half dozen teams to work on OAs, don't plan out how this work will be done in two years, and don't shoehorn people into all levels of Growth OS activities. Give the pilot a nine-month horizon, and keep your focus tight.

The goal of this first phase of work is simply to get everyone situated. Acclimating to new roles doing new work is awkward. You need to get the first group of eager New to Big teams comfortable, engaged, and up to speed before you can even consider taking these processes to the next level. Build one small, self-contained sandbox, and focus on making everyone who's playing in it feel like they've got a handle on things.

To build the sandbox, you'll need to get the lay of the land. Where will the sandbox be housed? Who will help build it? What resources do you have on hand to support it? In essence, your first steps in creating a pilot for New to Big work will focus on diagnostics and configuration.

PILOT DETAILS
Time frame: 6 to 12 months

CAPABILITY PRIORITIES: DIAGNOSTIC & CONFIGURATION

Align on pilot objectives—Make sure the leadership defines what success looks like.

Establish the Ops Team—Find your barrier busters and go-fast ninjas.

Introduce growth mind-sets and the OS framework—You need everyone working from the same playbook.

Pilot talent and funding models—Remember, do the easy thing that's good enough!

Identify internal capabilities and gaps—What do you have, and what do you need?

GROWTH PRIORITIES: DISCOVERY AND ESTABLISHMENT OF OAS

Growth Board: Enterprise-level—start with one GB at the top, owned by the CEO.

Ops Team: Enterprise-level—This team will become your internal experts at New to Big.

Opportunity Areas: 1 or 2—Start with just one or two in the pilot; there's time to expand later.

OA Teams: 2 or 3—Staff a few teams so that your pilot doesn't get sidetracked if one or two cofounders don't work out. (You can put more than one team against an OA.)

Focus on defining portfolio goals and metrics—How many bets do we want in motion, and what's the time horizon we're driving to?

Diagnose your starting point

To launch new businesses you need to have the capabilities to incubate those companies on a small scale. (That is, you need to get them from New to Big before you can take them from Big to Bigger.)

You likely already have some existing assets and capabilities to support this work. Instead of throwing it all out and starting from zero, you're better off taking stock of the people, resources, and networks your organization currently has to support innovation, and cataloging which mechanisms, people, and bits of existing infrastructure can be used for Growth OS work. For instance, you may already have prototyping capabilities, or a team of designers and developers you could commandeer to form a labs team. Or perhaps you have a forward-thinking lawyer or two who is absolutely delighted at the thought of streamlining processes for rapid in-market testing of new products and services. You also need to identify where the major capability gaps are, and create a road map to address them.

In addition to internal mapping, compile a resource list of external people and organizations who might be able to offer insights or assistance. Entrepreneurs who fall within the networks of your company's leadership, startups in the area or who are connected to your organization, possible academic partnerships, even nearby angel investors. At the very beginning, you'll be unsure which types of support you'll need to enable New to Big work, so build an arsenal of knowledge, allies, and experts. Alongside the Ops Team, these folks will be essential in clearing roadblocks and providing outside-in guidance to OA teams and the Growth Board.

Nothing is secret, nothing is sacred

The teams working on New to Big projects will live in their own separate sandbox. Many of the normal rules won't apply to them, they'll be held to different performance standards, and the work they'll be doing will be wildly different from everyone else's. They're special, different, set apart . . . and therefore both fascinating and threatening in equal measure to most promoters. Everyone outside the circle either wants to be inside, or at least to be *told* exactly what's going on inside. If they aren't, they may panic, complain, and resist.

As we discussed in chapter 8, it is essential that everyone understand what's going on. Installing the Growth OS is ultimately a process that happens across levels, in multiple business units, and it affects the whole company directly or indirectly. Failing to address pressing internal questions quickly, clearly, and empathetically means they'll multiply: more questions, more anxiety, more road-blocks, more wasted time. Additionally, treating everyone within the pilot like rock stars and everyone outside the pilot like peons causes rifts and breeds mistrust.

From what we've seen, the two biggest growth-killers are mis-aligned goals and misunderstanding. When different groups doing New to Big work have different ideas about why the work is being done at all, you end up with factions, friction, and shoddy results.

The best way to avoid that disaster is to communicate strategi-cally; no secrets, no elitist nonsense, no BS. Creating an effective communication strategy is critical to creating buy-in, building in-ternal alignment, and shaping the growth story of the organization, both internally and externally. And part of that strategy will be branding the work.

Why? Because it gives everyone a common language in which to discuss what's going on, ask targeted questions, and understand the answers they receive. Once it's branded, it's no longer viewed as a toy. It's a real growth program, which means people are more apt to respect it. So give it a memorable, branded name that reflects your specific company's personality and mission. Give it the gravitas it deserves.

Document now, teach later

Assuming the pilot is successful, you'll expand New to Big work beyond your initial teams and OAs, building it into a company-wide operating system for growth that touches every business unit. Unless you want to reinvent the wheel every time a new group is brought on board, you'll need to both document your processes and analyze the living daylights out of them.

Yes, everyone will experience the discomfort of transition; there's no getting around that bit. Over those first nine months, they'll try and fail and learn and regroup and pivot and tinker with new tactics. Finding and capitalizing on a new, viable business opportunity is one of the Ops Team's objectives, but being process-focused guinea pigs is another. They're living through this new methodology, identifying the kinks, and doing their best to work them out.

Those first teams should be able to teach the next cohort how to do New to Big work in ways that gel with your company's existing procedures, assets, goals, and people. And if there's no documentation of what worked, what didn't, and what wasn't even attempted, they'll have a seriously frustrating time doing it.

Doing the work is sexy. *Documenting and post-processing* the work is not. But if you do one without the other, you're setting yourself up for one-off success but expansion failure.

Go slow to go fast

Another benefit of documentation? It forces everyone involved to work slowly and mindfully, putting real thought into each step instead of sprinting forward and hoping for the best. The pilot phase—those first nine months—should be thoughtful and steady. Cross-country, not the fifty-yard dash. Select OAs, get a few quarters of Validation under your belt, and convene a couple of Growth Board meetings, but don't force more work into this time frame. The pilot is like a set of training wheels; its entire purpose is to build confidence, teach mechanics, and get everyone comfortable riding. Since every participant will learn at a different pace, getting them comfortable should be a gradual, thoughtful process. Although we want to foster quick decisions and fast learning *eventually*, we need to go slowly at the beginning to make that speed possible in the future.

One advantage of taking this work at a measured pace is it allows you to customize, course-correct, and pivot. You may find that some of the processes and recommendations we've outlined in this book really grind the gears of your company, and if they do, we encourage you to build workarounds.

For instance, maybe you've already done some exploratory work while researching current customer problems, and want to use the Growth OS to apply new thinking to existing projects. If that's the case, you can take a project that's already in motion, pause it, and reframe it as an OA. Look at it through the lens of customer pain points; ask, "What does this customer need, and how are we addressing that need with this product or service?" By recasting the project as an OA, you give the team permission to explore other possible solutions.

If you try to cruise through the first steps of the pilot at light speed, you'll miss out on key learnings and provide a painfully short adjustment period for your teams. Instead, get some early proof of the increased speed and decreased cost of learning through this approach. Allow the teams to open the aperture on new solutions they'd never have proposed before using the Growth OS methodology.

Phase 2: Expand into the business units

Once your initial teams have gotten their sea legs, demonstrated some real impact, and become comfortable enough with their new roles to start teaching others, it's time to spread the joy of New to Big deeper into the company. This next phase is especially important if you're focused on cultivating growth capability, since it disseminates this new knowledge base to a larger group within your organization, but also has value if you're still focused on net new growth. After all, there's only so much one or two OA teams can explore. If you're aiming for more bets overall, you'll need more teams doing the work.

Based on what's clearly worked within the pilot phase, decide what to replicate and what to abandon. Then start discussing both how to expand and which business units show the most promise for becoming New to Big powerhouses.

EXPANSION DETAILS
Time frame: 12 to 18 months

CAPABILITY PRIORITIES: EXPERIMENTATION AND LEARNING

Codified OS framework—The Ops Team documentation from the pilot needs to be cleaned up and codified into a framework of how the Growth OS works in your organization.

Established Validation methods, systems, and training—The methods and tools the cofounders use are codified and packaged up for training and replication with the next pool of cofounders.

Expand into new business units/geographies—As new BUs/geographies set up OAs, the Ops Team will need to expand their resources and processes to support them (for example, teams running experiments in Europe will require support from legal to comply with different privacy rules).

Human Systems "labs" in motion—The "good enough" workarounds that the HR/People Team used in the pilot shift into more formalized experiments and systems for talent.

Communications program—It's time to start sharing the work of the Growth OS more broadly within the organization.

GROWTH PRIORITIES: HEALTHY PORTFOLIOS

Growth Board: Enterprise-level + new business unit–level GBs—Now that your first GB is going strong, add Growth Boards at the BU leadership level for the business units you expand into.

Ops Team: Enterprise-level + new BU-level Ops support—Let the enterprise Ops Team teach BU-level Ops teams.

Opportunity Areas: 2 to 5 per BU—Just like in the pilot, start with a couple in new BUs and then add OAs over time.

Portfolio of solutions per OA (organic and inorganic)—Each OA should have a handful of active solutions in the seed stages, with an eye on inorganic (startup investment/partnership/acquisition) bets as well.

Ongoing recon to shape OAs—Recon isn't a one-and-done process; cofounders need to keep an eye on startup activity, investment flows, technology timelines, and regulatory changes that might shape or redirect OAs.

Stage the rollout carefully

Assuming you've branded this work and been enthusiastically communicative with the entire company about progress and successes, there are likely to be a few business units eager to hop on board and implement Growth OS methodologies themselves. That eagerness is fabulous, and definitely something you want in your Phase 2 participants . . . but eagerness alone is not enough.

You'll need to partner with business units that have both growth potential and proven stability. You're looking for groups that are doing fairly well at their current work—not ones struggling to meet revenue goals—so they have the funding and breathing room to try something new. And you need to work with groups that have some of the skills, knowledge, and foresight necessary to make New to Big work successful. Forward-thinking team members, growth-minded unit leadership, and flexible infrastructure are all necessary here. Enthusiasm is a must, but so is capability for experimentation. Pick your Phase 2 business units strategically.

Then create and run the equivalent of a pilot (Phase 1) within each unit. If you've got seven units primed and ready to rock, don't put them all into pilot at once; stage the rollout. Consider adding two units every six months so the expansion feels manageable, especially to the initial teams, who will be doing some heavy lifting as they teach their peers to fill new roles. If your Phase 2 teams have enough time to truly master this process, they can be enlisted to teach the next group of teams and let the Phase 1 gang off the hook. This is what building growth capability looks like: enabling more and more learning to be shared internally by more and more people. This is what will enable your Growth OS to be always on, always humming, always uncovering new business opportunities.

Diversify through inorganic growth

We haven't talked about your venture portfolio in a few chapters, have we? Time to revisit this key concept. Phase 2 is the perfect time to explore new ways to ensure that the bets you have running in every single OA are diversified, and that includes investing in, partnering with, and acquiring related companies.

The reason we haven't been peppering you with reminders to look outside your own walls for OA-supporting bets is that you need to start by building organic growth first. Build your Growth Board, master the Discovery and Validation processes, have a clear view of the OA playing field, and unleash a solution or two of your own before buying up the competition. If you don't, your partnerships will likely crush startups with Big to Bigger processes, your venture investments will be late and expensive, and your acquisitions will be dilutive at best and disasters at worst. Organic first, inorganic second.

Once you have a portfolio of organic bets and a validation-based understanding of the space, you should begin to think about M&A and venture investments. Which existing startups could you invest in to increase the volume of bets in your portfolio? Which companies could you buy who are building a validated solution within your OA? How can you partner with startups to learn quickly and cheaply together? In Phase 2, inorganic bets complement your organic teams.

Phase 3: Scaling the Growth OS

Once you've successfully replicated the Growth OS pilot within a few business units and you're seeing progress, you are ready to scale to the rest of the organization. What does that look like? We have some guidelines to share, but in general, this stage is different for each company because it is dependent on the ways you configured and customized the OS in the first two phases.

SCALING DETAILS

Time frame: 18 to 24 months

CAPABILITY OBJECTIVE: ENTERPRISE ROLLOUT

Deploy OS mind-sets + mechanics across enterprise—This is your opportunity to roll out the New to Big way of working to the rest of the organization, so they understand and value the work inside the Growth OS (and can apply the tools to their work when it is relevant).

Build a bench of coaches—The best cofounders from Phases 1 and 2 have the opportunity to step into a coaching role, serving as advisors to new cofounders when they enter the program.

Growth OS playbook to codify learnings—Take your codified New to Big systems and processes and create artifacts that teams can rely on as you expand.

Mature talent program (reporting, incentives, reviews, promotions)—Your HR systems for New to Big have graduated from "good enough" to repeatable, sustainable, and scalable.

GROWTH OBJECTIVE: LAUNCHING NEW BUSINESSES

Growth Board: enterprise-level + BU-level GBs across company—Each business unit has a Growth Board, and it is understood across the organization that this is the funding mechanism for new opportunities.

Ops Team: enterprise-level + BU-level OS support—Each BU has their own Ops Team to support the work within their group, and they share best practices and learnings with Ops Teams across the organization.

Robust portfolio of solutions per OA (organic and inorganic)—OA portfolios are healthy and Growth Boards see a robust pipeline of bets they can rely on for growth.

Launch of 4 to 6 businesses—Depending on the scale and speed of rollout, by this point the Growth OS should have graduated a handful of businesses through the build (beta) phase.

Creation of Build Incubator (systems, governance, talent, etc.)—By Phase 3 the "sandbox" should be formalized into an incubator with the systems, governance, and talent pipeline needed to take validated bets from the seed stages and build them as businesses.

Case Study: D10X at Citi

Scaling is *highly* individual and will vary depending on what your company does and how you are positioned in the market. But since it can be challenging to envision rollout without some concrete details, let's take a look at how Citi successfully scaled the Growth OS. The company has done a truly phenomenal job of taking the process through pilot, nurturing it, and installing it as a permanent growth capability across the company.

Citi has long been committed to bringing the outside in and innovating based on customer needs. In 2010, Citi Ventures was founded by the company's first chief innovation officer, Debby Hopkins. "Citi has two-hundred-plus years of expertise working with consumers, companies, and governments. From the very start we realized that to drive growth we needed to recast that expertise in new ways that are highly relevant to our customers. The question was how," Hopkins says.

Hopkins was stationed in Silicon Valley, where she built a team with diverse backgrounds in innovation and venture investing from companies including Apple, eBay, HP, Target, and venture capital firms. Venture investing gave Citi a ringside seat to disruption in action, where entrepreneurs were creating new business models and products. "But the missing piece was that, despite having a lot of activities going and great talent with relevant skills, at the end of the day innovation without impact doesn't count. And impact at an extremely large company requires methodology that can be shared across the organization. What was missing was a horizontal platform that would allow us to adopt a common way to create things and bring them to market across the enterprise."

In 2014, Hopkins was at an event hosted by investor Ben Horowitz when she ran into Beth Comstock, who, upon hearing her challenge, declared, "You need to meet David Kidder." A few days later, Hopkins called me just as I was waiting for a taxi at the San Francisco airport, headed into the city for a few days of meetings. "Hey, I need to meet you!" she said when I picked up the phone. Climbing into the car, I changed my route down to the peninsula and met her for dinner at the Fleet Street Café in Menlo Park. Over the course of the meal we sketched on the paper tablecloth the components of the Growth OS and dug into how Hopkins could adapt it for Citi's needs. Hopkins recalls the "aha" moment was when she recognized that Growth Boards were a way for the business units to own their innovation portfolios while leveraging a common growth operating system.

This realization that lasting impact inside an established organization requires a shared way of working led to the founding of D10X, a program managed by Citi Ventures, based on the Growth OS and named for its focus on discovering solutions that are ten times better for clients. (Yes!) The growth model allowed Citi to embrace innovation regardless of whether it was happening externally or internally and created the structure and safety necessary to support employees as they tested their ideas.

At the very beginning, the teams responsible for building D10X had more questions than answers, which is only natural. But they dove in fearlessly and launched six Growth Boards within the first year, then began training employees to hone, test, and pitch their ideas. They knew they'd have to evolve the program significantly over time—and they still continue to refine it, even today—but within those first twelve to eighteen months, much of the work felt fluid.

In 2016, Hopkins retired and Vanessa Colella was named chief innovation officer of Citi and head of Citi Ventures. "In terms of groundwork, David and the Bionic team were extremely helpful in framing for us the challenges of building new businesses while operating at the scale we do at Citi," explains Colella. "A fair share of that groundwork was a mind-set shift; framing the different orientation that's required when you're exploring a brand-new idea versus the orientation that's required when you're managing a business at scale. That was extraordinarily valuable to us in Citi Ventures and to our colleagues and leaders across the bank."

She also points out that in most cases, a company the size of Citi would likely postpone launch until they'd created a meticulous long-term plan, cultivated a sense of how many resources to hire, and gauged what kind of time commitment was needed.

"We did not do that for our internal startups, and that meant we made a lot of mistakes in the early going," she admits. "But we learned a lot and we collaborated extraordinarily closely with our colleagues in the businesses in order to shape D10X in a way that was valuable to their endeavors."

How did the D10X teams deal with those early setbacks and failures? Brutal honesty. They earned permission to make mistakes because they were open from day one about what they were trying to accomplish. They also remained mindfully open to feedback when things weren't working, and pivoted when change was necessary.

And how did D10X become a permanent, always-on growth machine running alongside Citi's corporate core? Well, time, trial, and error were all part of the process. At the same time that they were running the unit, advising employees, and nurturing their ideas, the company was actively collecting as much data and insight as it could about what was working and what wasn't, in order to propel the work forward. From the very beginning, Citi chronicled and analyzed D10X's work with the ultimate goal of understanding how to expand and scale it.

Cultivating a bench of experienced entrepreneur coaches also drove successful scaling.

"We've now hired close to two dozen former entrepreneurs who serve as coaches for our teams and cofounders," Colella says. "They help bring in real-world, gritty experience. They know what it's like to pitch to venture capitalists, what it's like to raise money, and how optimistic and passionate and humble you have to be to design a product."

These coaches help the D10X teams refine, validate, and test their ideas, but also mentor them in continually cultivating outside-in behaviors. They show the Citi employees how to be over-the-top passionate about their endeavors, while simultaneously re-maining extraordinarily empathetic and listening to signals from the marketplace. They know from experience that it's hard to know how to execute this work, and have been instrumental in teaching D10X participants to balance competing parts of their brains.

Finally, bringing innovation to scale was fueled by a dedication to shaping the future of finance, and widespread support for anything that improved Citi's customer service capabilities. The company was able to attract talent, leadership, and resources because of that shared attitude and outlook.

The company's leaders are quick to point out that D10X is quite culture-specific, and that effective tactics for Citi might not work at another company. But in regard to scale, Colella says that releasing the notion of singular ownership has also been instrumental in allowing Citi to expand its growth capability, and this mind-set shift might also benefit other organizations. She emphasizes both a team mentality of shared ownership and a commitment to trusting team members as they experiment and execute.

"The key to innovating at a company like Citi is enabling our employee base to innovate," she says. "It's akin to when your kid goes off to college; you hope that you've done everything to prepare them, but you really just have to let them go. That's how I think about D10X. We're not trying to scale a central program, we're trying to scale a way of problem-solving across the company. We engineered it that way from the beginning."

Citi is not trying to replace an existing business system through the work of D10X. The company has embraced the entrepreneurship plus VC model as a form of management for New to Big, but never sought to supplant their Big to Bigger operating system, which has been essential to making their growth work both sustainable and scalable.

Profile of a D10X Startup

D10X has successfully launched many startups, but one that's been particularly successful is Proxymity. It was founded by two Citi employees, Dean Little and Jonathan Smalley, who recognized that proxy voting is a cumbersome and antiquated process.

Quick overview of proxy voting: If you own stocks, at least once per year you'll receive a giant, imposing packet of paperwork in the mail. The enclosed documents describe specific decisions the company wants to make with options for each. You, as a shareholder, are asked to vote via a paper ballot and mail it back. It is inevitably a lengthy and convoluted document that can stymie even the most informed of shareholders. Many recipients struggle to understand what to vote for, or even what they're voting on. Sophisticated institutional investors often hire third-party vote advisors to help them understand the specific agenda items and how to vote such that the decision aligns to the investor's values and interests. If you do vote, your ballot is then passed through several intermediaries before returning to the original organization. The process takes ages and has a high potential for introducing errors. It's also wildly expensive.

For Citi's institutional investor clients—who may oversee hundreds, thousands, or even tens of thousands of ballots on behalf of their clients—this process is deeply onerous. But individual investors still need to voice their input, especially in our current climate where corporate transparency is valued and investors want a say in the environmental, social, and governance decisions of the companies they're supporting.

The D10X team wanted to streamline the process while bringing real-time accuracy to this critical piece of corporate governance. They developed Proxymity as an online platform that connects companies more directly with shareholders. This tool allows investors to view a digital meeting agenda and vote digitally, thereby giving companies a clearer view of how shareholders are responding to company issues. The entire process is validated, and concludes with a post-meeting vote confirmation.

After identifying the confusing and inefficient nature of proxy voting as a customer pain point (Discovery), and experimenting to create a radically different solution (Validation), D10X developed and launched Proxymity in 2017. The startup is on track to support up to two hundred meetings in the UK throughout 2018.[2]

Proxymity is just one of nearly one hundred active startups across all of Citi's major businesses, and D10X will continue to launch more in the years to come. But while volume of businesses is a definite hallmark of success, the company also keeps a close eye on internal participation and enthusiasm as signs of progress.

Colella says she monitors things like "How many of our internal cofounders whose first startup failed will come back and want to do it again? How many groups want to hear about what's happening in D10X so that they might be able to participate? We're trying to gauge real-world signals of how much pull there is from everyone at the company, from leadership through to our newest employees who are participating in some way, shape, or form in the program."

D10X participants are encouraged to embrace productive failure, and report on learnings from what *doesn't* work as much as from what does. They're also encouraged to remember that any successes are built through a tremendous amount of bravery and tenacity across the whole company.

"It's a way of working and a way of thinking that requires a very long view in terms of what you're building," Colella says.

Anyone who tells you scaling will be easy is lying to your face. As this case study illustrates, developing your Growth OS work into a permanent growth capability will take time, experimentation, effort, and the ability to bounce back from a long string of failures. But as this case study *also* illustrates, devising a way to scale this work in a way that suits your specific organization can create an internal New to Big machine capable of spawning multiple revenue-generating startups *every single year*.

10

GO ON OFFENSE

THE BEST PREDICTOR OF ENTERPRISE NEW TO BIG SUC-cess has been something founders learn through the unrelenting grind of launching and scaling their startups: It all starts with the CEO's mind-set. We did not realize how rare it was to find a growth leader—someone who can reliably deliver New to Big businesses and net new revenue—at the top of a Fortune 500 enterprise until we saw it up close. To say we were alarmed would be a polite way to put it.

A bit of radical candor: If the CEO and their leadership team do not directly own and drive New to Big, growth will not happen. Period. Enterprises do not have a money, ideas, or talent problem; they have a leadership problem: leaders who fundamentally have lost the incentive and skill to discover and create growth as a permanent organizational capability.

In Jeff Bezos's annual letter to Amazon shareholders over the past twenty years, he's continually reinforced the importance of a "Day One" mind-set, and cautioned against becoming a "Day Two" organization. Why? Because, as a founder, he understands how critical it is that the entire organization, starting with him, preserve their entrepreneurial mind-set. That fear of complacency, of losing speed and grit and an appetite for risk as culture scales—it's what makes the company more like a scaled startup than a lumbering enterprise (and Wall Street has rewarded them for it).

On Day One, the hunger, passion, ability to adapt, and sheer energy are as strong as they will ever be, because that is what is required to survive. When you lose that core energy, you lose the ability to grow. Day Two is about stasis and irrelevance. Day Three is long and excruciating decline. In many cases, this may be your grand challenge as a CEO: to restore the "Day One" growth culture.

Which begs the questions: Are you playing to win? Or just playing not to lose? What's the difference? It turns out, quite a lot.

As captured in one of my favorite books on team leadership, *Top Dog* by Po Bronson and Ashley Merryman, in 2008, researchers Geir Jordet and Esther Hartman published a paper studying performance under pressure among professional soccer players during penalty shootouts.[1] In the study, they calculated the conversion rate of shooters in the final shot of a penalty shootout, comparing two scenarios: when the shooter's team was down by a goal (so the team would lose if the player missed the shot), and when the shooter's team was tied (so the team would win if the player made the shot).

Jordet and Hartman found that in the first scenario, when missing the kick would cause the team to lose, professional players converted 62 percent of those shots. However, when the conversion would result in a win, kickers were successful 92 percent of the time. It's the same kick, the same setup, the same distance; the only difference is the athlete's mind-set.

Playing to win means granting the full permission and investment to compete, even if the odds aren't in your favor. Playing not to lose, on the other hand? It's protecting an entitled culture of efficiency and derisking that is predominantly incentivized to avoid and obscure the consequences of failure.

Most organizations we meet are playing not to lose. As a result, "innovation" has become something of an empty buzzword. (We mostly avoid using the word *innovation* at Bionic because of the brain damage, baggage, and distrust that come along with it.) Even when an "innovation" team is given the mandate to crack open new opportunities and go after new solutions, technologies, or business models, their permissions and boundaries are narrow: Don't take any risks until we're sure we can win. Do the analysis, run the numbers, and create the twenty-year forecast so we can build consensus. Nothing launched means nothing failed, right?

Growth is radically different. Growth is urgent. Growth is grounded in commercial truth. Growth does not adhere to invisible permissions or restrictions. Growth is in the culture, or it's not. When you're honest with yourself, can you really say you're playing to win?

All the CEOs and teams we work with are experiencing the same complexities and changes in the world as you are, and they know the velocity of change is only increasing. They also know they don't get to opt out. By now we hope that you can see the cost of not installing and driving a permanent growth capability: the excruciating, painful decline of Day Three.

The good news is that you don't have to be able to predict the future in order to grow. You only have to enable your teams to go out and uncover it. So don't task an innovation team to go after technology-of-the-moment innovation theater; instead, commit resources to discovering and solving real customer needs and seeding a portfolio of bets to meet those needs. Don't send your corporate venture capital (CVC) team off to Silicon Valley to just chase startups and write inconsequential "strategic learning" checks; integrate

your CVC into your New to Big machine so that they can fund bets that actually *are* strategic and driving your OA portfolio. Don't fear the startups that are coming your way; go on offense and beat them at their own game. There is no monopoly on this model.

Startups won the first round of disruption as the Fortune 500 outsourced growth and innovation to the Valley. We believe enterprises can win round two. Why? Because you have some not-so-secret weapons in the battle for growth: loyal customers, massive distribution channels, manufacturing capabilities, scaling systems, and the brand equity that startups and venture capitalists can only dream of. You can accelerate a customer adoption curve that startups could never handle. You are in a position to not only see and meet the future, but to make the future happen sooner.

Startup founders get much of the attention these days, and a handful of successes like Jeff Bezos from Amazon, Sara Blakely from Spanx, and Elon Musk of Tesla/SpaceX offer the dramatic narrative and singular personality-driven visions that fuel the media machine. It can be tempting to look at founders with a mix of disbelief and awe (perhaps mixed with a touch of defensiveness and valuation envy) and insist that they get to play by a different set of rules. And as a leader of a large, existing organization you aren't a founder. It's true.

You can, however, be a *refounder*.

Refounders are leaders who—despite not having created their companies from scratch—adopt the Day One mind-sets and model of founders. As we noted in chapter 2, Microsoft's Satya Nadella is an excellent example of a refounder; when he took over the CEO role in 2014, he immediately began refocusing the entire enterprise on growth-centric endeavors.

"If you don't jump on the new," he proclaimed, "you don't survive."

Taking that philosophy to heart, Nadella challenged the company

to see beyond its legacy products and began investing in new technologies like AI and Software as a Service (SaaS). He positioned Microsoft to grow into a cloud-computing giant by launching Azure, and purchased LinkedIn to plug Microsoft services into the company's social graph, then acquired GitHub to reengage with the developer world as a partner, not an entangled customer.

Through it all, Nadella has emphasized the importance of a growth mind-set: long-term thinking, utilizing a test-and-learn approach, and obsessing over customer problems, needs, and outcomes. He's also given the company permission to learn from their failures, most notably with the Windows phone. "If you are going to have a risk-taking culture, you can't really look at every failure as a failure. You've got to be able to look at the failure as a learning opportunity," he told *Business Insider* in 2017.[2]

The market has rewarded his bold tactics and visionary mind-set: After years of stagnation, Microsoft has regained its place on the top-five market cap list. The market now grants it a growth company multiple.

Taking a page out of Nadella's book isn't as daunting a task as it might seem. The Growth OS creates a New to Big machine inside of existing organizations. This book is your manual for how to configure and install it alongside your Big to Bigger operation. Together, these dual operating systems give you the power to discover and validate new ideas at the speed and cost of startups, then launch the validated ideas into new businesses at the scale of enterprises.

Installing the Growth OS is your first giant step toward activating the future. You'll be igniting a cultural growth mind-set and upgrading your company for a prolific and permanent drive for growth. You'll be showing your peers, shareholders, employees, and competitors that you live as an ambidextrous leader—you have the ability to operate *and* create; you can win at Big to Bigger *and* New to Big.

Big used to beat little; today, fast beats big. Fortunately, you're now ready. You're done envying Silicon Valley, and eager to turn the tables and make *them* envy *you*. You're primed to go on offense and win big. It's time.

And perhaps more important, we need you to succeed. Your partners, customers, and stakeholders need you to succeed. We hope, at the very least, our book has convinced you to take on the grand challenges of our time. Your leadership legacy will be in transforming the will and capability of your organization to imagine and contribute to an equitable, accessible, and sustainable future. If a startup has an innovative idea, they have to scrape and claw to make their way. But if you have the same idea, you can throw your resources and scale behind it to make change happen instantly, whether that is using less water in your supply chain, decreasing the cost of renewable energy, or increasing the accessibility of financial services products.

Now is the time to take action. We believe in you.

David, Christina, and the Bionic team
david@onbionic.com
christina@onbionic.com

ACKNOWLEDGMENTS

This book would not have been possible without the friendship and insights of Beth Comstock, who fueled the creation of Bionic and ignited what became the Growth OS. Our deepest gratitude to Anne Berkowitch, cofounder of Bionic, sparring partner of David, and editor extraordinaire of early drafts of this book. Another early reader, Janice Fraser, gave excellent feedback on flow and punctuation alike, along with being a major content contributor to the later chapters on people and teams. And Susan Green made (and continues to make) everything happen—masterfully crafting David's schedule and ensuring we could squeeze in interviews and writing time between his work of running Bionic and being a dad and husband.

Thank you to the Bionic entrepreneurs, venture partners, product managers, ethnographers, analysts, and account managers past and present who contributed content from their experiences inside the Growth OS: Godfrey Bakuli, Leslie Bradshaw, Margot

Brassil, Greg Brody, Katie Chanpong, Owen Davis, Maxine Friedman, John Geraci, Viv Goldstein (who first started working with us during her GE days building FastWorks), Danielle Hildebrandt, Hanny Hindi, Caroline Hribar, Emma Imber, Dennis Jones, Lyndsay Katz, Juliette LaMontagne, Abigail Rogers-Berner, Stephanie Schott, Kevin Schroeder, Kimberly Skelton, Graham Smith, Janice Semper, Rick Smith, Ariel Steinlauf, and Katie Tilson. Thanks as well to the Bionic Labs team for incredible design and web development support: Zayne Abraham, Tess Dennison, Eric Freitag, Jordan Kerzee, Bronson McKinley, and KJ Zeitlian.

We also need to thank our partners for going on this journey with us, and a few, in particular, who have made incredible contributions to the development of the Growth OS: Lindsey Argalas, Nina Barton, Chip Bergh, Chris Boeckerman, Debbie Brackeen, Carlos Brito, Ana Botin, Terri Bresenham, Vanessa Colella, Mike Corbat, Christopher Crane, Pedro Earp, Kathy Fish, Eric Gebhardt, John Gerspach, John Hart, Tim Hockey, Brian Hoff, Debby Hopkins, Kate Johnson, Hannah Jones, Carey Kolaja, Jud Linville, Robert Locke, Tim Noonan, George Oliver, Patrick O'Riordan, Mark Parker, Julie Setser, Lorenzo Simonelli, David Taylor, and Jack Thayer.

Thank you to our advisors, who consistently push our thinking and help us level up as we grow: Sunny Bates, Randall Beard, Mark Bonchek (the man who originally coined the phrase "New to Big"), Bruce Brown, Pauline Brown, Adam Grant, Susan Lyne, Gen. Stanley McChrystal (Ret.), Gautam Mukunda, Wendy Murphy, Eric Ries, Jim Stengel, and Jeff Walker.

Nick Beim, Tim Chang, Chris Dixon, Roger Ehrenberg, Brad Feld, Chris Fralic, David Hirsch, Rick Heitzmann, Reid Hoffman, James Joaquin, Eric Paley, Chris Sacca, David Tisch, and Albert Wenger all were generous with their time and hard-won learnings as veteran investors, providing interviews and follow-up material throughout the research process. And finally, an immense debt of gratitude to Christina's writing partner and research assistant, Sally McGraw. (If you're writing a business book, you'd be smart to hire her assistance.)

Thanks to our partners at Currency, Roger Scholl and Tina Constable, plus their fabulous teams. And we'd be remiss if we didn't give a special thanks to Joy Tutela at the David Black Agency. Joy is the kind of agent a writer dreams of. Thanks for going on this crazy journey yet again.

Wherever the book falls short, we offer our apologies in advance. And wherever you highlighted insights or took notes in the margins on learnings to share, it is likely the result of the collective wisdom and work of the people on these pages.

Finally, we owe a huge thank-you to our families for putting up with the many disruptions to family life and supporting us through this endeavor. To Johanna Zeilstra, and Jack, Stephen, and Lucas Kidder, thank you for creating the space and grace to discover who we are all becoming, for granting the permission to live out a purpose, at the expense of moments of belonging together. (I love you all so profoundly.) And to Chas Carey and our plants Odo de Carelace and Wort, Christina loves you more than she ever thought possible.

GLOSSARY

10x: A solution that is exponentially ("ten times") better than whatever solution the customer currently uses.

ambidextrous leader: A leader who is both a skilled operator within the existing business and a creator of new businesses; someone who can lead in both Big to Bigger and New to Big.

beachhead customers: A specific customer segment to win over first, before expanding the product or service offerings to the wider world.

cofounder: A member of an Opportunity Area team; an enterprise intrapreneur.

commercial truth: Truth that is supported by evidence, often uncovered by testing and observing customer behavior ("do") rather than trusting in surveys ("say").

Executive Sponsor: A senior executive who guides a co-founder team, pushing their thinking, encouraging the rigor of validation work, and removing roadblocks.

External Venture Partner (EVP): An experienced entrepreneur and early-stage investor who brings an outside creator's independent perspective on startup opportunities to the Growth Board.

Growth Board: The guiding body that's set up within an organization that can approve, fund, and champion bets. It is, essentially, a venture fund that invests in enterprise entrepreneurs and manages a growth portfolio of bets.

Opportunity Area (OA): An area of growth opportunity discovered at the intersection of new customer behaviors and needs and new technologies and trends.

Ops Team: The group of creative problem-solvers who are responsible for driving and scaling the Growth OS within their organization.

players and **promoters:** Players are those who are "all-in" in the Growth OS, like co-founders. Promoters are those who are merely involved with the Growth OS, but who are critical in facilitating the work of the players, such as supporting functions like marketing or finance.

proprietary gift: An organization's unique capabilities that can be leveraged toward growth.

Total Addressable Market (TAM): The amount of the market demand for a product or service that a company can reasonably capture (or "address").

Total Addressable Problem (TAP): The estimated demand to solve a problem in a radically new way if a hypothetical solution were to exist at an accessible price point.

zombies: Projects that suck up talent and resources because no one at an organization can kill them without navigating difficult politics, facing judgment, or jeopardizing careers.

NOTES

CHAPTER 2

How We Got Here

1. Steven Pearlstein, "How the Cult of Shareholder Value Wrecked American Business," *Wonkblog* (blog), *Washington Post*, September 9, 2013.

2. Roger L. Martin, "The Age of Customer Capitalism," *Harvard Business Review*, January 2010.

3. Clayton M. Christensen, "A Capitalist's Dilemma, Whoever Wins on Tuesday," *New York Times*, November 3, 2012.

4. Robert W. Patterson, " 'Whatever's Good for America . . . ,' " *National Review*, July 1, 2013.

5. John Kenneth Galbraith, *The New Industrial State* (Boston, MA: Houghton Mifflin Company, 1967).

6. Pearlstein, "How the Cult of Shareholder Value Wrecked American Business."

7. Martin, "The Age of Customer Capitalism."

8. David Graeber, *The Utopia of Rules* (New York: Melville House, 2015).

9. Martin, "The Age of Customer Capitalism."

10. Pearlstein, "How the Cult of Shareholder Value Wrecked American Business."

11. World Bank, "Stock Market Turnover Ratio (Value Traded/ Capitalization) for United States [DDEM01USA156NWDB]," retrieved from FRED, Federal Reserve Bank of St. Louis, January 31, 2018, https://fred.stlouisfed.org/series/DDEM01USA156NWDB.

12. Richard Parker, *John Kenneth Galbraith: His Life, His Politics, His Economics* (Chicago: University of Chicago Press, 2006), 613.

13. "Stock Market Turnover Ratio (Value Traded/Capitalization) for United States [DDEM01USA156NWDB]."

14. Clayton M. Christensen and Derek van Bever, "The Capitalist's Dilemma," *Harvard Business Review*, June 2014.

15. Six Sigma, "The History of Six Sigma," https://www.isixsigma.com/new-to-six-sigma/history/history-six-sigma/.

16. Six Sigma, "The Importance of Six Sigma Training," https://www.sixsigmaonline.org/six-sigma-training-certification-information/the-history-and-development-of-six-sigma/.

17. Christensen and Bever, "The Capitalist's Dilemma."

18. Martin, "The Age of Customer Capitalism."

19. Ben Geier, "What Did We Learn from the Dotcom Stock Bubble of 2000?," *Time*, March 12, 2015.

20. "The Dot-Com Bubble Bursts," *New York Times*, December 24, 2000.

21. Kurt Eichenwald, "Microsoft's Lost Decade," *Vanity Fair*, July 24, 2012.

22. Sarah Green Carmichael, interview with Satya Nadella, "Microsoft's CEO on Rediscovering the Company's Soul," September 28, 2017, *HBR IdeaCast* (podcast), *Harvard Business Review*, https://hbr.org/ideacast/2017/09/microsofts-ceo-on-rediscovering-the-companys-soul.

23. Nilay Patel, interview with Satya Nadella, "The Future of Microsoft with Satya Nadella," *Verge Video*, The Verge, October 7, 2015, https://www.theverge.com/video/2015/10/7/9473677/microsoft-windows-10-device-event-satya-nadella-interview.

24. Bob Evans, "Microsoft's Soaring Growth in the Cloud Makes Marc Benioff's Digs Seem Silly," *Forbes*, November 13, 2017.

25. Larry Fink, "A Sense of Purpose," annual letter to CEOs, https://www.blackrock.com/corporate/en-us/investor-relations/larry-fink-ceo-letter.

26. Harvard Kennedy School, "Julie Battilana Says It's Time to Understand How to Maximize Social Value," Winter 2018, https://www.hks.harvard.edu/research-insights/policy-topics/social-innovation-philanthropy/julie-battilana-says-its-time.

27. Eric Ries, *The Startup Way: How Modern Companies Use Entrepreneurial Management to Transform Culture and Drive Long-Term Growth* (New York: Currency, 2017), 12.

CHAPTER 3
From TAM to TAP

1. Aswath Damodaran, "Uber Isn't Worth $17 Billion," FiveThirtyEight, June 18, 2014.

2. Bill Gurley, "How to Miss by a Mile: An Alternative Look at Uber's Potential Market Size," *Above the Crowd* (blog), July 11, 2014, http://abovethecrowd.com/2014/07/11/how-to-miss-by-a-mile-an-alternative-look-at-ubers-potential-market-size/.

CHAPTER 4
The Growth Leader Challenge

1. Jeff Desjardins, "Here's How Commercial Drones Grew Out of the Battlefield," *Business Insider*, December 14, 2016.

2. Anton Wahlman, "Tesla Doesn't Even Have a Model 3 Beta Prototype Yet," *Car and Driver*, March 2, 2017.

3. WD-40, "History: Fascinating Facts You Never Learned in School," https://www.wd40.com/cool-stuff/history.

4. Benedict Evans, "In Praise of Failure" (blog), August 10, 2016, https://www.ben-evans.com/benedictevans/2016/4/28/winning-and-losing.

5. Vahid Monadjem, "Be Good at Being Wrong by Getting It Right Quickly," *Entrepreneur Magazine*, June 25, 2015, https://www.entrepreneurmag.co.za/advice/starting-a-business/launch/be-good-at-being-wrong-by-getting-it-right-quickly/.

6. *National Geographic*, Genographic Project, "The Development of Agriculture," https://genographic.nationalgeographic.com/development-of-agriculture/.

7. "The Creed of Speed," *Economist*, print edition briefing, December 5, 2015.

8. Robert McMillan, "Turns Out the Dot-Com Bust's Worst Flops Were Actually Fantastic Ideas," *Wired*, December 8, 2014.

9. Julie Wainwright, "Former Pets.com CEO: Here's the Real Reason the Company Blew Up," *Business Insider*, February 3, 2011.

10. Kristin Wong, "Why It's So Hard to Admit You're Wrong," *Smarter Living* (blog), *New York Times*, May 22, 2017.

11. Paul Randolph, "Why Being Wrong Really Hurts," *Guardian* (UK), February 28, 2016.

12. Judith E. Glaser, "Your Brain Is Hooked on Being Right," *Harvard Business Review*, February 2013.

13. Ana Swanson, "How to Convince Someone to Change Their Mind, According to Science," *Independent* (UK), February 11, 2016.

14. Larry Johnson and Bob Phillips, *Absolute Honesty: Building a Corporate Culture That Values Straight Talk and Rewards Integrity* (New York: AMACOM, 2003), 112.

15. Gaylin Jee, "What Is Your Company's Mindset Orientation?" (blog) 33 Emeralds, March 30, 2017, https://thirtythreeemeralds .com/2017/03/30/what-is-your-companys-mindset-orientation/.

16. John Battelle, "Getting Past 'Addicted to Being Right'—Bringing the Outside In at Citi," *Shift* (blog), NewCo, September 6, 2018, https://shift.newco.co/getting-past-addicted-to-being-right-bringing -the-outside-in-at-citi-1102930da843.

17. Ben Horowitz, "Lead Bullets" (blog), Andreessen Horowitz, November 12, 2011, https://a16z.com/2011/11/13/lead-bullets/.

18. David Sturt, "Creativity: How Constraints Drive Genius," *Groupthink* (blog), *Forbes*, July 12, 2013.

19. Stav Ziv, "A Brief History of SpaceX," TechCrunch, January 20, 2016, newsweek.com/spacex-timeline-brief-history-reusable-rocket -launches-417944.

20. Chris Dixon, interview with Eric Ries, "Eric Ries on 'Vanity Metrics' and 'Success Theater,'" TechCrunch, September 24, 2011.

21. James G. March, "Exploration and Exploitation in Organizational Learning," *Organization Science* 2, no. 1 (February 1991), http:// www.analytictech.com/mb874/papers/march.pdf.

22. Interview with Fidji Simo, "How Facebook's VP of Product Finds Focus and Creates Conditions for Intentional Work," *First Round Review*, http://firstround.com/review/how-facebooks-vp-of-product -finds-focus-and-creates-conditions-for-intentional-work/.

CHAPTER 5

Discover a Big, Unmet Customer Need

1. Rita Gunther McGrath, "The Pace of Technology Adoption Is Speeding Up," *Harvard Business Review*, November 25, 2013.

2. Stanford d.school, "Extreme Users," http://dschool-old.stanford .edu/wp-content/themes/dschool/method-cards/extreme-users.pdf.

3. Dale Buss, "Consumers Want More Product Customization, But Manufacturers May Not Be Able to Deliver," *Chief Executive*, July 31, 2018, https://chiefexecutive.net/consumers-want-more-product -customization-but-manufacturers-may-not-be-able-to-deliver/.

4. Steven Zeitchik, " 'Black Panther' Will Break Box-Office Records. But Will It Change the Movie Business?," *Chicago Tribune*, February 16, 2018.

5. Mariama Sow and Amadou Sy, "Lessons from Marvel's Black Panther: Natural Resource Management and Increased Openness in Africa," Brookings, February 23, 2018, https://www.brookings.edu /blog/africa-in-focus/2018/02/23/lessons-from-marvels-black -panther-natural-resource-management-and-regional-collaboration -in-africa/.

6. Carvell Wallace, "Why 'Black Panther' Is a Defining Moment for Black America," *New York Times Magazine*, February 12, 2018.

7. "Silicon Valley Gets a Taste for Food," *Economist*, print edition, Technology Quarterly, March 5, 2015.

8. Benedict Evans, "Ways to Think About Market Size," (blog), February 28, 2018, https://www.ben-evans.com/ benedictevans/2015/2/28/market-size.

9. Morgan Brown, "Airbnb: The Growth Story You Don't Know," Growth Hackers, September 4, 2014, https://growthhackers.com /growth-studies/airbnb.

10. Biz Carson, "How 3 Guys Turned Renting an Air Mattress in Their Apartment into a $25 Billion Company," *Business Insider*, February 23, 2016.

11. Ibid.

12. Ibid.

13. Ibid.

14. Brown, "Airbnb: The Growth Story You Don't Know."

15. Ibid.

16. Ibid.

17. "Experiences" tab, Airbnb.com, https://www.airbnb.com/s /experiences.

18. Leigh Gallagher, "Airbnb CEO: Here's How 'Experiences' Are Doing So Far," *Fortune*, October 23, 2017.

19. Ibid.

20. Ibid.

CHAPTER 6

Validate Like an Entrepreneur

1. Tonya Garcia, "Amazon's Aggressive Warehouse and Shipping Strategy Is Paying Off," MarketWatch, January 10, 2017, https:// www.marketwatch.com/story/amazon-has-taken-convenience-to-a -new-level-and-its-hurting-offline-rivals-2017-01-09.

2. Lauren Goode, "Tons of People Are Buying Fitbits, but Are They Actually Using Them?," The Verge, August 6, 2015, https://www.theverge.com/tech/2015/8/6/9110035/fitbit-fitness -tracker-watch-active-users-sales.

3. Julia Lurie, "What We've Suspected About Fitbits All Along Is True," *Mother Jones*, October 4, 2016.

4. Nike, Easy Kicks program, https://www.easykicks.com/.

5. "How a Pitch in a Neiman Marcus Ladies Room Changed Sara Blakely's Life," *How I Built This* (podcast), NPR, September 12, 2016, https://www.npr.org/templates/transcript/transcript .php?storyId=493312213.

CHAPTER 7

Invest Like a VC

1. Seth Levine, "Venture Outcomes Are Even More Skewed Than You Think," *VCAdventure* (blog), August 12, 2014, https://www .sethlevine.com/archives/2014/08/venture-outcomes-are-even-more -skewed-than-you-think.html.

2. Chris Dixon, "Performance Data and the Babe Ruth Effect in Venture Capital" (blog), Andreessen Horowitz, June 8, 2015, https://a16z.com/2015/06/08/performance-data-and-the-babe-ruth -effect-in-venture-capital/.

3. Robert H. Hayes and William J. Abernathy, "Managing Our Way to Economic Decline," *Harvard Business Review*, July–August 2007.

4. Interview with Adam Grant, "'Originals': How Anyone Can Become a Trailblazer," *Knowledge@Wharton* (podcast), February 2, 2016, http://knowledge.wharton.upenn.edu/article/how-non-conformists-move-the-world/.

5. "You May Need a Stranger on Your Portfolio Review Committee," Viewpoints on Innovation, August 17, 2010, http://viewpoints.io/entry/you-may-need-a-stranger-on-your-portfolio-review-committee.

CHAPTER 9

Install a Permanent Growth Capability

1. Clayton M. Christensen and Stephen P. Kaufman, "Assessing Your Organization's Capabilities: Resources, Processes, and Priorities," module note (Boston: Harvard Business Publishing, 2008).

2. Press release, "Citi and Computershare Collaborate to Launch Innovative Digital Platform for Proxy Voting," BusinessWire, June 28, 2018, https://www.businesswire.com/news/home/20180628005883/en/Citi-Computershare-Collaborate-Launch-Innovative-Digital-Platform.

CHAPTER 10

Go on Offense

1. G. Jordet and E. Hartman, "Avoidance Motivation and Choking under Pressure in Soccer Penalty Shootouts," *Journal of Sport & Exercise Psychology* 30, no. 4 (2008): 450–457.

2. Krzysztof Majdan and Michał Wasowski, "We Sat Down with Microsoft's CEO to Discuss Past, Present and Future of the Company," *Business Insider*, April 20, 2017.

RESOURCES

EXECUTIVE MIND-SETS FOR GROWTH

Books

Hit Refresh: The Quest to Rediscover Microsoft's Soul and Imagine a Better Future for Everyone, Satya Nadella, Greg Shaw, and Jill Tracie Nichols

Imagine It Forward: Courage, Creativity, and the Power of Change, Beth Comstock and Tahl Raz

Team of Teams: New Rules of Engagement for a Complex World, General Stanley McChrystal, Tantum Collins, David Silverman, and Chris Fussell

Top Dog: The Science of Winning and Losing, Po Bronson and Ashley Merryman

Uncommon Service: How to Win by Putting Customers at the Core of Your Business, Frances Frei and Anne Morriss

Unleashing the Innovators: How Mature Companies Find New Life with Startups, Jim Stengel and Tom Post

Whiplash: How to Survive Our Faster Future, Joi Ito and Jeff Howe

Talks

"Listen, Learn . . . Then Lead," Stanley McChrystal, https://www.ted
.com/talks/stanley_mcchrystal

"The Power of Experimentation," Scott Cook https://www.youtube.com
/watch?v=Z0vA6Bsuew0

ENTREPRENEURSHIP

Books

Lean Analytics: Use Data to Build a Better Startup Faster, Alistair Croll
and Benjamin Yoskovitz

Lean Customer Development: Build Products Your Customers Will Buy,
Cindy Alvarez

*Lean Startup: How Today's Entrepreneurs Use Continuous Innovation to
Create Radically Successful Businesses*, Eric Ries

Sprint: How to Solve Big Problems and Test New Ideas in Just Five Days,
Jake Knapp and John Zeratsky

*The Startup Owner's Manual: The Step-By-Step Guide for Building a
Great Company*, Steve Blank and Bob Dorf

*The Startup Playbook: Secrets of the Fastest-Growing Startups from Their
Founding Entrepreneurs*, David Kidder

*The Startup Way: How Modern Companies Use Entrepreneurial
Management to Transform Culture and Drive Long-Term Growth*, Eric
Ries

Ten Types of Innovation: The Discipline of Building Breakthroughs, Larry
Keeley, Helen Walters, Ryan Pikkel, and Brian Quinn

TALENT AND PEOPLE

Books

The Alliance: Managing Talent in the Networked Age, Reid Hoffman, Ben
Casnocha, and Chris Yeh

*Emotional Agility: Get Unstuck, Embrace Change, and Thrive in Work and
Life*, Susan David

Good People: The Only Leadership Decision That Really Matters, Anthony
Tjan

Grit: The Power of Passion and Perseverance, Angela Duckworth

Measure What Matters: How Google, Bono, and the Gates Foundation Rock the World with OKRs, John Doerr

The Power of Habit: Why We Do What We Do in Life and Business, Charles Duhigg

Quiet: The Power of Introverts in a World That Can't Stop Talking, Susan Cain

Radical Candor: Be a Kick-Ass Boss Without Losing Your Humanity, Kim Scott

Start with Why: How Great Leaders Inspire Everyone to Take Action, Simon Sinek

Talks

"The Surprising Habits of Original Thinkers," Adam Grant, https://www.ted.com/talks/adam_grant_the_surprising_habits_of_original_thinkers

"Why the Best Hire Might Not Have the Perfect Resume," Regina Hartley, https://www.ted.com/talks/regina_hartley_why_the_best_hire_might_not_have_the_perfect_resume

"Why the Secret to Success Is Setting Good Goals," John Doerr https://www.ted.com/talks/john_doerr_why_the_secret_to_success_is_setting_the_right_goals

"People, Leadership, and Startups," Bill Campbell, https://youtu.be/GHLg1wDuc10

DESIGN THINKING
Books

Change by Design: How Design Thinking Transforms Organizations and Inspires Innovation, Tim Brown

Creative Confidence: Unleashing the Creative Potential Within Us All, Tom and David Kelley

The Design of Business: Why Design Thinking Is the Next Competitive Advantage, Roger L. Martin

The Field Guide to Human-Centered Design: Design Kit, IDEO.org

Insight Out: Get Ideas Out of Your Head and into the World, Tina Seelig

Make Space: How to Set the Stage for Creative Collaboration, Scott Doorley, Scott Witthoft, and the Hasso Plattner Institute of Design at Stanford University

Thinking in Systems: A Primer, Donella H. Meadows

The Three-Box Solution: A Strategy for Leading Innovation, Vijay Govindarajan

The Undoing Project: A Friendship That Changed Our Minds, Michael Lewis

VC MIND-SETS AND PRACTICES
Books

Blitzscaling: The Lightning-Fast Path to Building Massively Valuable Companies, Reid Hoffman and Chris Yeh

High Growth Handbook, Elad Gil

The Masters of Private Equity and Venture Capital: Management Lessons from the Pioneers of Private Investing, Robert Finkel and David Greising

Messy Middle: Finding Your Way Through the Hardest and Most Crucial Part of Any Bold Venture, Scott Belsky

The Shareholder Value Myth: How Putting Shareholders First Harms Investors, Corporations, and the Public, Lynn Stout

Smart People Should Build Things: How to Restore Our Culture of Achievement, Build a Path for Entrepreneurs, and Create New Jobs in America, Andrew Yang

The Startup Game: Inside the Partnership between Venture Capitalists and Entrepreneurs, William H. Draper III

Thinking in Bets: Making Smarter Decisions When You Don't Have All the Facts, Annie Duke

Venture Capitalists at Work: How VCs Identify and Build Billion-Dollar Successes, Tarang and Sheetal Shah

Zero to One: Notes on Startups, or How to Build the Future, Peter Thiel and Blake Masters

Books

Exploration & Exploitation in Organizational Learning, James March

The Innovator's Dilemma: When New Technologies Cause Great Firms to Fail, Clayton M. Christensen

Originals: How Non-Conformists Move the World, Adam Grant

Teaming: How Organizations Learn, Innovate, and Compete in the Knowledge Economy, Amy C. Edmondson

INDEX

Note: *Italic page numbers* indicate glossary references.

ABOUT THE AUTHORS

DAVID S. KIDDER is an entrepreneur and an angel investor in more than thirty companies. He is the cofounder and CEO of Bionic, which unlocks new growth and competitiveness for the world's largest enterprises based on the models, methods, talent, and tools of venture capital and entrepreneurship. Previously, Kidder served as the cofounder and CEO of Clickable and cofounded SmartRay Network. A graduate of the Rochester Institute of Technology, he received Ernst and Young's Entrepreneur of the Year Award in 2008. He is the creator and coauthor of the *New York Times* bestselling series The Intellectual Devotional and the author of *The Startup Playbook*. He lives in Westchester County, New York, with his wife and three sons.

CHRISTINA WALLACE is the Vice President of Growth at Bionic and the cohost of the podcast *The Limit Does Not Exist*. A serial entrepreneur, Wallace previously founded BridgeUp: STEM, a computer science education startup at the American Museum of Natural History; was the founding director of Startup Institute New York; and was the cofounder and CEO of Quincy Apparel. She holds undergraduate degrees from Emory University and an MBA from Harvard Business School. She lives in Brooklyn with her husband, Chas Carey, and their two plants.